theatre & migration

Theatre&
Series Standing Order ISBN 978–0–230–20327–3

You can receive future titles in this series as they are published by placing a standing order. Please contact your bookseller or, in case of difficulty, write to us at the address below with your name and address, the title of the series and the ISBN quoted above.

Customer Services Department, Macmillan Distribution Ltd, Houndmills, Basingstoke, Hampshire, RG21 6XS, UK

theatre & migration

Emma Cox

palgrave
macmillan

First published 2014 by
PALGRAVE MACMILLAN

Palgrave Macmillan in the UK is an imprint of Macmillan Publishers Limited, registered in England, company number 785998, of Houndmills, Basingstoke, Hampshire RG21 6XS.

Palgrave Macmillan in the US is a division of St Martin's Press LLC, 175 Fifth Avenue, New York, NY 10010.

Palgrave Macmillan is the global academic imprint of the above companies and has companies and representatives throughout the world.

Palgrave® and Macmillan® are registered trademarks in the United States, the United Kingdom, Europe and other countries

ISBN: 978–1–137–00401–7 paperback

This book is printed on paper suitable for recycling and made from fully managed and sustained forest sources. Logging, pulping and manufacturing processes are expected to conform to the environmental regulations of the country of origin.

A catalogue record for this book is available from the British Library.

A catalog record for this book is available from the Library of Congress.

Printed in China.

contents

series editors' preface

The theatre is everywhere, from entertainment districts to the fringes, from the rituals of government to the ceremony of the courtroom, from the spectacle of the sporting arena to the theatres of war. Across these many forms stretches a theatrical continuum through which cultures both assert and question themselves.

Theatre has been around for thousands of years, and the ways we study it have changed decisively. It's no longer enough to limit our attention to the canon of Western dramatic literature. Theatre has taken its place within a broad spectrum of performance, connecting it with the wider forces of ritual and revolt that thread through so many spheres of human culture. In turn, this has helped make connections across disciplines; over the past fifty years, theatre and performance have been deployed as key metaphors and practices with which to rethink gender, economics, war, language, the fine arts, culture and one's sense of self.

Theatre & is a long series of short books which hopes to capture the restless interdisciplinary energy of theatre and performance. Each book explores connections between theatre and some aspect of the wider world, asking how the theatre might illuminate the world and how the world might illuminate the theatre. Each book is written by a leading theatre scholar and represents the cutting edge of critical thinking in the discipline.

We have been mindful, however, that the philosophical and theoretical complexity of much contemporary academic writing can act as a barrier to a wider readership. A key aim for these books is that they should all be readable in one sitting by anyone with a curiosity about the subject. The books are challenging, pugnacious, visionary sometimes and, above all, clear. We hope you enjoy them.

Jen Harvie and Dan Rebellato

foreword

None of us are the picture in our passport. When a border guard looks at us for ten seconds or for ten minutes, who do they see? What in the computer file that they consult as they pass your documents through their system at a checkpoint would begin to say anything about the courage, the love, the vision, the generosity, or the potential of the human being who stands in front of them?

Theater is a contribution to the necessity of deepening those ten seconds of vision and revealing the inadequacy of the documentation. And it is about challenging the furtive and presumptuous look of the culture of surveillance with the eye-to-eye meeting of equal beings. The urgent and timely imperative is to mount a direct challenge to the ingrained and totalizing gaze of white supremacy, which has determined that people who look a certain way and come from certain countries have the right to travel and an unlimited economic horizon, while people who look another way and come from other countries will have no right to travel and will never be allowed to participate on an equal economic footing.

Every culture on Earth has primary and foundational myths, legends, and stories which understand that in order to find yourself, you have to leave your own country and your own people and go to a distant land where you will be challenged, amazed, and transformed and where, in adversity, you will meet your hidden heroic self and find friends you never imagined you would have. It has long been understood across cultures and across civilizations that none of us are who we appear to be to our immediate family and friends and that it is only in a far-away place that we begin to discover other selves, other possibilities that lie within us.

Our new era of borders and hyper-legal immigration and deportation superstructures has criminalized one of the most basic human yearnings, one of the most basic ways in which human beings complete themselves, one of the most basic ways worlds open, eyes open, and hearts open. We are living in a period of shame in which human beings are referred to as "aliens" and deportations are discussed as "removals," as if a person is a piece of furniture or a can of garbage. This dehumanization of nomads, travelers, searchers who are equipped with the courage and tenacity to leave everything that is comfortable behind and to venture against all odds into the unknown looking for change and willing to sacrifice everything for it – the dehumanization of the very flower of humanity demeans the species. It lowers all of our sights, blunts and tempers the courage of all of us, and shrinks our native generosity into a sad space of selfishness, fear, and mistrust.

The ten percent of the world that is consuming eighty percent of the world's resources cries out that we don't have enough to go around, and that we have to be protected from the invasion of hungry foreigners. On the other hand, we have every right to visit their countries whenever we please, and anything we want there is ours for the taking. In the United States, it is not an accident that 241,493 individuals (out of 357,422) "removed" in 2013 were from Mexico, because one-third of the United States was originally Mexico, and Spanish remains the majority language in many communities – these are migration patterns that have persisted across centuries. The new criminalization treats as a criminal offense each border crossing, so that people who come back again and again are not recognized as following in the footsteps of generations of ancestors, but as seasoned criminals who are now guilty of multiple felonies. Special courts have been set up in the borderlands with Mexico which convict people crossing through the desert as criminals, each person being given a twenty-five-second hearing and verdict. They are shipped from their twenty-five-second hearing directly to one to six years of incarceration in a for-profit US prison and immediately deported upon completion of their sentence.

Human beings trying to solve problems with purely negative and legalistic means are capable of creating unspeakable atrocities and miscarriages of justice. The entire grim procedure which creates thousands of fresh criminals every afternoon goes relentlessly forward, smashing families and enforcing and reinforcing racist stereotypes with the shrill fanfares of self-righteousness and law and order jargon that accompany periods of repression all over the globe.

(But aliens are not aliens; they are people. And in the process of turning people into aliens we have actually become alienated from ourselves.)

The little book you are holding treats a range of theatrical projects that have undertaken to challenge and to interrogate immigration procedures and policies across the world in the last generation. Different productions in different contexts have opted for different strategies. Some works speak from positions of power and privilege, while others speak from the perspective of those whose human rights and whose humanity have been called into question. Some productions compose their questions in front of well-groomed and influential audiences at major festivals; others have been seen by determined audiences of friends, enemies, and activists in basements, abandoned parking lots, and in front of detention centers. This small book treats many strategies in many situations, with particular attention to North America, Australia, and New Zealand, where policies are particularly harsh. I'm grateful that this book exists and I am interested and gratified by the range of histories, options, and invention surveyed in these pages.

Ongoing solutions to the permanent challenge posed by immigration and migration in the twenty-first century demand the best from all of us. The timeless aspects of the dilemma have been inflamed and made desperate by the unprecedented, sweeping, and systematized political and economic violence of the "new world order," which has been unmatched in any previous century. The solutions will have to be creative solutions. And humane solutions. Which is why the humanities must be present and active. It is hopeful and humbling to see creative people engaging the question.

(The act of making theater is the act of recognizing, affirming, extending, imagining, and re-affirming a community or, possibly, communities. Metaphorically at first, and then literally and tangibly, theater is the creation of newly shared space on Earth.)

Peter Sellars is a theater, opera, and festival director and a professor in the Department of World Arts and Cultures at UCLA, USA. His productions include The Children of Herakles, *which toured Europe and the United States, working with refugee and immigrant communities, border guards, immigration judges, and public officials in each location.*

theatre & migration

Politics and mythopoetics

It is 1939, the brink of the Second World War. A hot evening. In the garden of an elegant home on the island of Tasmania, a charity performance is unfolding: the host, a middle-aged woman, is playing the exiled Iphigenia, daughter of Agamemnon and Clytemnestra, stationed as priestess at the temple of Artemis at Tauris, where she must condemn all strangers to death. As this Australian Iphigenia stands amid crumbling (but not ancient) marble columns and recounts a terrible dream about the ruin of her ancestral home in Argos, an interloper in far-flung Tauris/Tasmania is brought to her to be sacrificed. Iphigenia does not at first recognise her brother, the shipwrecked Orestes, played by the host's husband. In the next scene, set the following morning, a blind guest to the house stumbles upon the imitation temple and is disoriented by the echo of his footsteps on marble in the Australian environment.

He explains afterwards to his concerned hosts: 'I was lost. I thought I was dead.'

Euripides' *Iphigenia in Tauris* (Theatre of Dionysus, Athens, *c*.414–412 BCE) bookends playwright Louis Nowra's landmark work *The Golden Age* (Playbox Theatre, Melbourne, 1985), serving as both play-within-a-play and askew mythology. Iphigenia's words of sympathy for Orestes and his cousin Pylades, '[y]ou surely have sailed long and far to this land; and long will you rest abroad in the earth below' (ll. 480–81, p. 103), or in Nowra's version, '[y]ou will die in pain and lie in an unmarked grave' (p. 94), prefigure the trauma that is about to be visited upon Australian society: a cataclysmic war for which tens of thousands of its people will travel half-way round the world to die far from home.

The Golden Age plugs into another mythology with its story of a 'lost' tribe discovered in the Tasmanian wilderness, the inbred and dying descendants of a band of escaped convicts and other misfits of the colonial past. 'Nowt more outcastin', the forest people's mantra, remembers the pain of their ancestors' exile (cast out first from Britain, then from colonial society), while their failure to thrive offers up the frightening prospect that a strand of Australia's migrant bloodline was rotten at the core. And inasmuch as the forest tribe may be read as an allegory for the Tasmanian Aboriginal population, obliterated by settler colonialism, the rupture of exile is ghosted by its inverse counterpart: the rupture of invasion and genocide.

This book concentrates on mid- to late-twentieth-century and contemporary theatre and performance engaged with stories, conditions and experiences of migration, though in doing so it traces migration histories and theatrical practices that are older than this. Even when we exclude its non-human forms, 'migration' is a word that encompasses a lot. What we can say is that whether it is thought of in terms of individuals (immigrant, expatriate, temporary worker, exile, refugee, itinerant, cosmopolitan nomad, et cetera) or collectives (colonial settlement, diaspora, slave or convict transportation, trafficking, displacement), migration is, at its heart, about encounters with foreignness – with foreign people, and with foreign places. These are, it may be supposed, ingredients of good storytelling.

But what do we mean by 'foreign'? Does 'foreign' simply refer to the geographical fact of coming from elsewhere? Or does it imply a stranger? In her book *Strange Encounters: Embodied Others in Post-Coloniality* (2000), Sara Ahmed warns against taking for granted that being a migrant consigns one to being a 'stranger', noting that it is 'relationships of social antagonism that produce the stranger as a figure in the first place' (p. 79). The unlucky 'strangers' who arrived before Orestes and Pylades at Tauris in Euripides' play are, it seems, aptly named in modern translations.

Migrants and strangers are also, of course, produced by movements through space. The work of Michel de Certeau gives us a useful starting point for thinking about these. In the chapter 'Spatial Stories' from *The Practice of Everyday Life* (1984), he conceptualises *place* as physical environment and *space* as human practices, relations and perceptions within it – or more succinctly: *'space is a practiced place'* (p. 117; italics in original). Remembering Ahmed's insistence that we don't just assume that 'migrant' = 'stranger', we see that it is only in de Certeau's *spaces* that migrants become *strangers* (that's not to say that migrants cannot themselves feel *strange* regardless of whether they encounter anybody else). *The Golden Age* can be deciphered as a palimpsest of spatial relationships to place: a layering of arrivals and departures, the result of involuntary migrations back and forth between Britain and Australia, and between suburban civilisation and wilderness. De Certeau argues that on a fundamental level, '[e]very story is a travel story – a spatial practice' (p. 115). The 'spatial syntaxes' (p. 115) of storytelling, he suggests, are not separate from life, but 'carry out a labor' (p. 118): stories 'make the journey, before or during the time the feet perform it' (p. 116). Language orders the interplay of place and space.

In theatre, we find particular footholds for comprehending de Certeau's philosophical account. Theatre about migration opens up bodily lexicons, as well as spatial syntaxes. Bodies on stage (or in the classroom, or on the street, or wherever else performance happens) actualise stories with a voice, accent, skin and history. So the cross-casting of Aboriginal Australian actors as Nowra's forest people, speaking the bawdy, Cockney- and Gaelic-inflected language the playwright invented for them, would flag up a very different roadmap of travel, kinship and dislocation stories than the casting of Australian actors of English, Irish, Welsh or Scots heritage. Oftentimes, theatre of migration pays attention to imagining the contact zone between those who arrive and those who lay claim to ownership or custodianship over a territory. But who does the imagining? Some of the work discussed in the following pages was written, produced or performed by migrants, while some of it comes from artists working in their natal environments (this includes the second-, third- or further-generation descendants of migrants as well as indigenous people).

An excavation of the authorial origins of iconic narratives of exile, journeying or pilgrimage for the purpose of comparison with today's theatre makers would be a largely unhelpful exercise. What matters is whether and how these and other recognised narratives – the *Ramayana*, the *Book of Exodus*, *Medea*, *Iphigenia in Tauris*, *Oedipus the King* and *Oedipus at Colonus*, *Journey to the West*, *The Divine Comedy*, *The Wandering Jew*, *As You Like It*, *The Tempest* – influence the way we tell and hear migration stories. I'm aware that reeling off this mini-list generates slippages and conflations between the religious and the secular, between myth, drama and verse, between European and Asian, not to mention slippages of more than a millennium. My discussion here is concerned more with the *cultural and political uses* of mythic or canonical material than with the particularities of its mode and content.

In relation to the uses of myth, Jean-Luc Nancy offers valuable insights. In the chapter 'Myth Interrupted' from his book *The Inoperative Community* (1991), Nancy states that '[m]yth is always the myth of community, that is to say, it is always the myth of a communion' (p. 51). By this he doesn't mean that myths are always *about* community, but that in the act of telling they gather people, igniting co-investment; in the context of theatre, the value of myth as a gathering, collectivising force is clear. For Nancy, what myths do matters more than what they consist of: 'we know that although we did not invent the stories … we did on the other hand invent the function of the myths that these stories recount' (p. 45). Part of what myths do, Nancy suggests, is embed power: '[w]hat is "mythic status"? What privileges has a tradition of thinking about myth attached to myth … ?' (p. 48). This is especially interesting in the context of Nancy's key claim, that modern and postmodern societies 'no longer live in mythic life' and 'have no relation to the myth of which we are speaking' (p. 52). Given this 'interruption', what is myth – and canonical texts, which are frequently the vehicles for myth – doing in contemporary theatre of migration?

The first section of this book develops this question in relation to the languages, stories, artists and audiences of theatre of migration. (I'm using the phrase 'theatre of migration' as shorthand for a range of theatre and performance that is responsive to different contexts of migration.) A concern with the politics of myth-making or mythopoetics persists throughout the second and third sections of the book, 'The Migrant Nation' and 'The Migrant City', but in these sections I am most interested in situating the nation (and nationhood) and the city (and urban identity) as sites as well as *ideas* with which theatre of migration is continually in conversation. In the second section the discussion turns briefly to the partition of India and its consequences, before concentrating on the settler colonial (sometimes termed 'settler invader') nations of Australia and New Zealand, while the third section takes as its case studies the cities of London, Cape Town and Toronto.

This structure is, obviously, one of innumerable ways in which a discussion on theatre and migration might proceed. The organising principles that I employ will, inevitably, highlight particular aspects of migration and of performance practice, while marginalising or obscuring others. 'Migration' is a big, unwieldy word with which to follow this book's ampersand, one that manifests in diverse and complex historical, social and cultural contexts. A migrant can be a person who leaves one home and makes another, or one with multiple homes, or none, or a person who eschews geographical fixity altogether. Migrants can be individuals, families or political communities. They may move by choice or by compulsion. They may be made welcome or shunned. And each of these contingencies can bleed into another.

While the main emphasis of this book is mid- to late-twentieth-century and contemporary theatre informed by histories of migration that also engages with migration as a topic or trope, it is important to locate the emergence of conditions of its possibility in the popular itinerant and immigrant theatres of the nineteenth century, which didn't necessarily foreground stories of migration. Theatrical trade routes mapped economic ones in the era of European imperial expansion and consolidation, with theatrical managers such as Maurice E. Bandmann and J. C. Williamson, actor-writer-managers such as Dion Boucicault and actors such as Julius Knight, Charles and Ellen Kean, Ira Aldridge, Oscar Asche and Lily Brayton establishing successful – and profitable – transnational careers spanning Europe, the United States, Canada, Australia, New Zealand, India, Southeast and East Asia and Africa (in relation to work in Australasia, see Veronica Kelly's 2011 book *The Empire Actors*, and for details of Bandmann's international career, refer to the Global Theatre Histories project, led by Christopher Balme at the Ludwig Maximilian University of Munich). Russian imperial geopolitics prompted theatrical migrations over a similar period: from the late nineteenth century to the mid-1930s, Yiddish theatrical troupes, compelled by persecution and by economic pressure in Russia and Eastern Europe, travelled to Western European cities and to New York, offering a range of popular musical, vaudeville and dramatic entertainments and in some cases playing a role in the development of theatrical Expressionism and Modernism (see David Mazower's 1987 book *Yiddish Theatre in London* and Nahma Sandrow's *Vagabond Stars: A World History of Yiddish Theater*, 1995). While imperial-era popular theatres were dominated by a repertoire of European plays and operas and European forms (melodrama gradually making room for Naturalist, Expressionist and Modernist work), some distinctly hybrid forms emerged out of colonial contact, such as the popular Malay-language, Eurasian musical theatre that toured the Dutch East Indies, detailed by Matthew Isaac Cohen in *The Komedie Stamboel: Popular Theater in Colonial Indonesia, 1891–1903* (2006). If itinerant and immigrant practitioners didn't tend to make migration their topical focus, the cultural and economic transactions initiated by their work represent the beginnings of theatre's globalisation as we recognise it today. These artists' careers also show how theatre and migration can be mutually propelling activities.

The post-imperial consciousness with which Nowra imbues *The Golden Age* – characterised by an awareness of shifting local and international affiliations – can trace its inheritance directly (if not solely) to the migrations and cultural transplantations that gave rise to imperial and colonial theatres. I offered the example of Nowra's play at the start of this book not to make a case for the enduring relevance of ancient Greek theatre and mythology, but because it offers a good place to begin thinking about how a play can enfold ancient ideas about exile, so that meaning, and indeed *meaningfulness*, derives from this enfolding, even as it opens up tensions between the ancient and the contemporary. If theatre of migration can both shape and reflect a society's imaginings of its 'others', then these imaginings are always already caught in an echo chamber of archetypal, often heroic, narratives. Certain mythic cornerstones – the painful separation, the journey, the encounter with others, the longing for home and, sometimes, the nostos (homecoming or return) – tend to prevail as far as the *emotional legibility* of migrant narratives is concerned. To put it another way, we already have a symbolic system by which we *recognise* (the Latin etymology is 'know again') migrants and migration, and this compels our reading of the political present.

We also have ways of recognising migrants laid out for us by bureaucracies. One of the most pressing questions we need to ask about the relationship between theatre and migration today, and a key component of this book's focus, is what migrants are made to mean under contemporary capitalism – it seems unwise to call it 'late' – when belonging is rationalised (and rationed) via an arsenal of passports, visas, body scanners and biometrics. It is from this rationalisation that formal categories of non-citizen emerge: highly skilled migrant (designated in the United States as an individual with 'Extraordinary Ability', and in the UK under various 'Tier 1' categorisations: 'Exceptional Talent', 'Entrepreneur', 'Investor' and 'General'), temporary worker, family migrant, student, unauthorised asylum seeker, refugee and so on. Each category carries an associated moral tinge, occupying a higher or lower rung on the ladders set out by what Homi Bhabha calls 'surveillant culture[s]' interested in differentiating 'the good migrant from the bad migrant' (*The Location of Culture*, 1994, p. xvii). We are living in a contradictory time in which capital moves more freely – many would argue more recklessly – around the globe than ever, while human movement, even in its increasing numbers, is subjected to closer scrutiny and codification. Theatre that has something to say about this has something to say about our global era.

What I'm calling a 'mythopoetics' of migration – literally 'making myth' out of migration – describes an accumulation of visions of foreignness that have collided in the globalised, bureaucratised present. Migrants exemplify the new in terms of mobility and adaptability (qualities that may, depending on circumstance, have everything or nothing to do with autonomy, choice or wealth) but are also frequently made recognisable – *communally*, Nancy might add – by way of mythologies about exiles or strangers extracted from the distant past. In other words, today's migrants are *of their time*, their documented or undocumented selves politicised by their border crossings, and yet they are known, at least in part, *out of their time*. The readiness with which exile (surely the most romanticised of migration's categories) can be flattened by a telescopic view of history is indicated by the opening sentence of a recent book on exile and literature: 'Exile is a phenomenon with a very long history: from Anaxagoras and Ovid to the recently exiled intellectuals, displaced persons, and refugees' (Agnieszka Gutthy, *Exile and the Narrative/Poetic Imagination*, 2010, p. 1). Of interest to me in this sentence is not that exile, like migration generally, is *an old thing*, but that the mythic weight of ancient stories pushes in on the present, entangling the economic and political conditions of contemporary mobility with transhistorical ideas about value or status. So we have to ask what might be the politics of mythopoetics in theatre of migration. What I'm getting at is: how and for whom is a mythopoetics of migration functional, and how and for whom is it dysfunctional?

Languages

In this book, I discuss mainstream and minor text-based drama, musical theatre, physical theatre, circus, dance, participatory theatre, documentary and site-specific performance, state-sponsored spectacle, and festivals, as well as political activism. In their capacities as theatres of migration, each can perform incisive cultural work that stems from the languages that are used – or absent. Some tools for reading these works can be derived from intercultural theatre scholarship, though I tend not to characterise them as 'intercultural', given that the word's implied designation of discrete cultures is prone to reifying relationships and artistic sources into an either/or. Nevertheless, some of the key issues at stake in intercultural theory and practice inform my reading of theatre of migration, and particularly its languages: mismatches of intention, methodology and perception, ideas about intellectual, cultural or spiritual property and the risk of decontextualisation, appropriation and commodification. In contexts of migration, to use a language is to transmit meaning across cultures and to unsettle semantics, and these are things that happen in nexuses of power – differences of culture, nation, class, race and gender – as well as over sometimes vast stretches of time and space.

Language and accent can have complex and often multiple effects in theatre of migration. They mark the performing body just as powerfully as skin: both may be political, as well as personal. A useful illustration of this can be found in Veronica Needa's autobiographical solo work *FACE* (Hong Kong Arts Centre, 1998), directed by Tang Shu-wing, which traces her family's British Hong Kong Eurasian history. Combining text-based and playback theatre, *FACE* was commissioned for Hong Kong's Festival Now, whose 1998 theme, 'Invisible Cities' (borrowed from Italo Calvino's evocative title), aimed at providing a forum for Hong Kong's marginalised and minority communities, including Filipino and Indian migrant workers and the Eurasian community. Needa describes the markedly different sensations and emotional consequences of performing for Hong Kong audiences in her half-forgotten mother tongue of Cantonese in comparison to English, the language of her literacy and daily life. The process of re-learning Cantonese was, Needa recalls, 'excruciatingly difficult and slow', like 'returning to a kind of infancy' (*FACE: Renegotiating Identity through Performance*, 2009, p. 17), but it eventually led to 'a visceral pleasure in delivering the Cantonese text. ... the text became much more integrated into body memory' (p. 18). Later performances of *FACE* in Britain (Lumley Studio, University of Kent, 2006) were more fully bilingual, the text reoriented to take account of broad national tastes. Metaphors in the two languages shifted in accordance with, on the one hand, a British predilection for irony (and general distaste for earnest sentimentality), and on the other, a more sentimental Hong Kong Chinese disposition: '[t]he metaphor of "moving" through honey being "sweet but thick" – in English with an edge of irony; becomes "immersed" in honey, "sweet enough to enter the heart" in Cantonese – directly sentimental' (p. 16).

In her essay 'The Home of Language: A Pedagogy of the Stammer' (2003), on migrant subjectivity and the attempt 'to locate a home within language ... which is not one's first language' (p. 41), Sneja Gunew describes the shift from one's birth language to the language of one's adult life (and, crucially, of literacy) in terms of displacement. This may or may not involve geographical migration; Gunew discusses the fragility of dialects and patois among certain diasporic groups where requirements to converse in a dominant language override contexts for using the first language: '[t]hose who aspire to the cultural capital of the dominant language ... are doomed to hear these first languages as disabled tongues, as lingual impediments, a stammering spasm in the midst of sleek, global rhythms' (p. 52). Noting that the stammer or stutter is traditionally taken to indicate 'disabled access to speech' (p. 44), Gunew investigates the potential for such quirks to productively destabilise cultural certainties, revealing heterogeneity (including foreignness) within language groups. For Needa, re-learning also had the creative affect of 'visceral pleasure'. While Cantonese cannot be called a minor dialect, it was for Needa the language of babyhood, of hired nannies, not the sphere of literacy or of Eurasian culture. Nor was it a language she used with her father. Delineations of social class, gender and ethnicity were woven into Needa's voicing of Cantonese on the Hong Kong stage in ways that were not as apparent in Britain.

This transnational example demonstrates several points about language and bilingualism. Perhaps most importantly, it shows us that language on stage can *contain* meaning without necessarily *conveying* meaning to an audience. In this regard, the politics of language in theatre is a complex thing: at once public and private, manifest and invisible, depending on the codes and competencies with which audiences are equipped to read a performance.

Stories

When a mythic or canonical model for imagining migrants and migration narratives is folded into contemporary theatre, we should ask how the model feeds the new work (and endorses its participants), and vice versa. An interesting case study for applying these questions is a production of *Pericles* (The Warehouse, London, 2003) co-created by the Royal Shakespeare Company and London theatre company Cardboard Citizens, which works with homeless and formerly homeless people, including asylum seekers and refugees. Directed by Adrian Jackson, the founding artistic director of Cardboard Citizens, *Pericles* was presented by a mixed cast of RSC actors and performers from refugee backgrounds. An interweaving of refugee testimonies with the Jacobean text, itself co-authored by Shakespeare, fleshed out equivalences between the two. Obviously, on one level, the production ran the risk of obscuring the particularities and urgencies of today's refugee politics: Pericles is not one of a generic many, but a privileged individual, temporarily exiled from his exulted position. But certain resonances were striking: the birth at sea of Pericles' daughter, Marina, for instance, was echoed in the story of a refugee born at sea. Moreover, the interpenetration of a Renaissance retelling of classical heroism and struggle with the supposedly insignificant stories of individuals living on the margins of contemporary society emblematised a commensurate right to be heard.

Certainly, the work's development was oriented around telling and listening: several months prior to the full-scale staging, an edited-down *Pericles*, presented by a mixed company of five, toured to London refugee support centres. Performances were followed by invitations to share stories, and selected individuals were followed up and interviewed. The resulting testimonies, along with those of the late Amal Basry, a survivor of the disastrous *SIEV X* sinking of 2001, in which 353 asylum seekers drowned in international waters south of Java (see Emma Cox, 'Territories of Contact', 2012), were integrated into the production at The Warehouse. This performance space, located in Southwark, was deliberately evocative of a detention centre akin to Calais's now-closed Sangatte and was the site of the previous year's Crisis at Christmas event for the homeless. *Pericles* was an ambitious promenade work that used several vast interiors, including an entry zone where audiences could peek into tents and see performances of testimonies on TV screens; a room set up like a forbidding exam hall in which audience members, seated at desks, were confronted with convoluted refugee application forms; a fisherman's shore overflowing with pegged clothing and washing machines; an austere arrangement of blue camp beds; and a Temple of Diana dominated by a bright, kitschy image of the late Princess Diana. The potential for the mix of Shakespearean drama and refugee testimony to produce uncritical pieties was undercut by lines that invited audiences to think critically about both as modes of representation. Interrupting a series of testimonies spoken in the exam hall (none of which, it should be noted, were the performers' own stories), a formally dressed man came forward to pronounce, '[t]hose are all the stories we have time for. Now, in future, please try to avoid stories which are too long, too complicated, too difficult to believe, too culturally specific, or too painful to listen to.' He was followed by a teacher figure who 'educated' the audience about how universal Shakespeare is.

Premiering the same year as *Pericles*, famed intercultural theatre director Ariane Mnouchkine's *Le Dernier Caravansérail (Odyssées)* (Théâtre du Soleil, La Cartoucherie, Paris, 2003) invoked the metonymic figure of wandering and nostos, Homer's Odysseus. In one of four notes for the programme, Mnouchkine's collaborator, Hélène Cixous, discursively gathered a collective mythic consciousness: '[i]n the beginning of our memories there was War. The *Iliad* told the story. After the War: *The Odyssey*. Those who did not return home, neither living nor dead, wander across the entire earth' ('Notes', 2005). A grander affair than *Pericles* in terms of budget and ticket price, if not space, Mnouchkine's five-hour epic toured to Quimper, Bochum, Lyon, Berlin, New York, Melbourne and Athens between 2004 and 2006. The work was broken into two parts, *Le fleuve cruel* ('the cruel river') and *Origines et destins* ('origins and destinies'), and its numerous vignettes drew upon Mnouchkine's and her colleagues' interviews and correspondence with asylum seekers, displaced people and trafficked women. Characters were from around the world and spoke various languages (translated via surtitles). Non-illusionistic devices – visible dressing rooms, billowing sheets representing a swollen river then a vast ocean, and low-wheeled platforms on which actors and sets glided into and out of view – were employed alongside the realism of snippets from recorded interviews and naturalistically acted scenes located in the contemporary moment: official immigration interviews, detention camps (Calais's Sangatte and Sydney's Villawood), Eurotunnel and airport chaos.

With its geo-cultural sweep, its vast assortment of characters and its use of conventions such as the illicit love affair, the cruel victimisation of underdogs and the dangerous escape, *Le Dernier Caravansérail* became a kind of mythopoetics of the dispossessed. In *Performance, Ethics and Spectatorship in a Global Age* (2009), Helena Grehan weaves Cixous's philosophical framing of the production, particularly her reservations about the use of 'spectacle to "seduce", "clothe" and to reveal the difficult and painful experiences of refugees', into a discussion of 'the limits of emotional responsiveness or empathy' (p. 118). Grehan considers the risk that a work which (as she shows) provoked some rapturous responses from reviewers 'will return the focus to spectators, instead of hearing and responding to the call of the other' (p. 128). In a similar vein, Helen Gilbert and Jacqueline Lo contend that the show 'infuse[d] the harrowing traumas communicated by the refugee stories with the aesthetic pleasures of orientalism' (*Performance and Cosmopolitics*, 2007, p. 205).

Another peculiar kind of pleasure haunted the work. Its repetitive focus on acute fear and pain (one woman's whipped, lacerated back; another's cowering sobs), orientalist or not, offered what Susan Sontag calls the 'pleasure of flinching' (*Regarding the Pain of Others*, 2003, p. 37). And at times, trauma trumped veracity: there was some fudging of history in a dramatic scene at sea in which Australian Special Air Service (SAS) personnel aboard a helicopter blared out a retreat order to a flimsy people-smuggling vessel. Australian maritime operations do include interception and return, but only once have the elite SAS been deployed: their infamous 2001 boarding of the freighter *MV Tampa*, whose Norwegian captain had rescued 438 asylum seekers. This event was summarised in the production's programme. *Le Dernier Caravansérail*'s 'truths', such as they were, were packaged so as to engineer deep emotional responses to extreme situations in much the same way as myths do. But as Jean-Luc Nancy reminds us (*The Inoperative Community*, pp. 53–54), most of us don't think that our myths are true in quite the same way.

And who is the collective 'we' that 'our' myths gather and speak to? Greek myths aren't necessarily (or even, usually) the first point of reference for artists who have experienced forced migration or are descended from forced migrants. Produced by London-based British Asian theatre company Tara Arts, *2001: A Ramayan Odyssey* (England tour, 2001) was directed by company co-founder Jatinder Verma. The play set out to imagine the crossroads of the sacred Hindu text and Greek myth. A small company of performers presented portions of the *Ramayana* with the figure of Homer's Odysseus present as a spectator who would occasionally interject to ask Rama questions about his decisions; then the same performers reversed the scenario, before the two heroes and their wives finally came face to face.

In *Global Diasporas* (2008), Robin Cohen, citing political theorist Bhikhu Parekh, argues that the *Ramayana* became a vital narrative among the Hindu diaspora in the nineteenth and early twentieth centuries in the European colonies in Africa, the Caribbean, and island territories in the Indian and South Pacific Oceans where they were transported as indentured labourers (Verma is himself a Tanzanian-born migrant who came to Britain from Kenya as a teenager during the Asian 'exodus' that followed Kenyan independence). Cohen contends that the centrality of the *Ramayana* in the diaspora occurred because:

> First, the book's central theme was exile, suffering, struggle and eventual return – a clear parallel with the use of the Bible by religious and Zionist Jews. Second, the text is simple and didactic, with a clear distinction between good and evil, a useful simplification in the harsh world of the plantation. Third, the *Ramayana* hammered home what the Brahmins and many conservative men wanted to hear. The eldest son should be dutiful, wives should be demure and obedient and clear roles should be defined for family interactions. Finally, as Hindu traditions go, the *Ramayana* was relatively casteless, but it especially stressed the virtues of the lower

castes, namely physical prowess and economic resourcefulness. (pp. 66–67)

Verma was aware of the stakes involved in his *Ramayan Odyssey*. He explains that one of the reasons the production was 'incredibly frightening' to create was the iconic status of the *Ramayana* in the Indian diaspora: 'we revere this text, it's come down to us for two thousand or more years' ('"Braids" and Theatre Practice', 2001, p. 133). But he also knew that engaging with the *Odyssey* would be strategic, furthering Tara's aim of including in touring schedules locations that aren't particularly ethnically diverse. He describes being 'faced with venue managers who say, "Oh well, there are no black people, no Asians, in my city, so what's point of seeing this?" Then you have to work with ruses. You say, oh, actually I'm bringing the *Odyssey*. "Oh well, that's alright. Come in with the *Odyssey*. No problem"' (p. 134). By invoking towering mythologies from 'East' and 'West' of exile, trial/adventure and return, Verma sought a balance between religious, cultural, artistic and economic interests – but not one so delicate that it would plaster over what he calls the 'abrasions' (p. 130) of multicultural contact.

Whether the *Ramayan Odyssey* 'gathered' a community in the way that Nancy tells us myth, by definition, must is another matter. Nancy explains: '[t]he very idea of inventing a myth ... is a contradiction in terms. Neither the community nor, consequently, the individual (the poet, the priest, or one of their listeners) invents the myth: to the contrary, it is they who are invented or who invent themselves in the myth' (*The Inoperative Community*, pp. 58–59). Verma's deliberate hybridising of existing myths is not the same as the creation of a new myth, but the *Ramayan Odyssey* is of less significance for its constitution of what might be termed a 'mything' community than for its (re)packaging of myth. It exemplified the kinds of intersections between myth, heritage, status and national identity that can propel theatre of migration.

Artists

Something that has been crucial, though perhaps implicitly, to this discussion so far is what we might call the 'politics of position': questions about how power affects opportunities for participation, especially authorship and directorship. It is important to attend to how theatres of migration differ depending on whether they are made by migrants, or by locals, or by some combination of these subject-positions. None is owed a moral monopoly on the use of migration as a dramatic trope, but there can be different interests at work when 'outsiders' are written and performed into being by 'insiders', as contrasted with 'outsiders' enacting some kind of self-representation.

Mythopoetics in the context of migration concerns not just the stories that are (re)told but also the way artists are positioned and perceived, whether by their own volition or by the desires of collaborators, audiences, critics and sponsors. The mythologising of individuals is sustained by aesthetic interests in difference (or 'strangerness', as Sara

Ahmed terms it), but it also comes down in large part to the persistent trope of the artist's condition as one of self-exile or estrangement. This understanding of what it means to be exiled is, typically, less concerned with transnational or intercultural politics than with existential questions and the relationship of the self to society. As Svetlana Boym notes with reference to Russian literary Modernism, 'the theory of estrangement and actual exile do not necessarily go together' ('Estrangement as a Lifestyle', 1996, p. 517). In *Performing Exile, Performing Self* (2012), Yana Meerzon brings geographical exile to the fore while maintaining the exile–estrangement–artist triad. She sets out to 'redefin[e] the exilic paradigm as a creative opportunity for the liberation of self' and 'celebrate the existential condition of being "other"', in order to 'shift the perception of exile away from the archetype of suffering, disorientation, and displacement, but also to explore the spiritual quest of the exilic artists who long to re-establish their creative environment and build an aesthetic shelter in a new land' (p. 8). Ahmed is less disposed than Meerzon to theorise estrangement or exile in terms of existential freedom, given the tendency for such understandings 'to conceal how estrangement marks out particular bodies and communities' (*Strange Encounters*, p. 93) by generalising it as a feeling common to all humans, much less all artists.

With some migrant artists, being a conduit for mythologies associated with geographical origin, life trajectory and complicated allegiance does not sit comfortably. In his essay 'The Theatricality of Religious Rhetoric: Gao Xingjian and the Meaning of Exile' (2011), Alexander C. Y. Huang describes Nobel Laureate Gao Xingjian's distaste for self-orientalisation among diasporic Chinese artists:

> Gao observes that the Chinese diasporic artists often sell Chinese 'antiques' that fuel and reinforce essentialized views of cultural difference. Gao criticizes the opportunist tendency, writing that 'an artist ... does not need to sponge a living off [his] ancestors [chi zuzong de fan]. ... He should not sell himself as a local product or handicraft [tu techan]'. (p. 369)

The idea of exile that Gao prefers is one of apolitical artistic liberation. His experimental work *Snow in August* (National Theatre, Taipei, 2002) was based on the life of Dajian Huineng, the illiterate Sixth Patriarch of Chan (Zen) Buddhism and a symbol of enlightenment through detachment. Written and directed by Gao, *Snow in August* drew on a number of dramatic, operatic, dance and acrobatic forms and was, according to Huang, 'a meditation on freedom and Gao's own ideological investment in the necessity of exile' (p. 367). Gao's cherished artistic freedom is, nevertheless, umbilically linked with the fact of his geopolitical exile from China and, since 2000, tangled up in the strings attached to his prestigious Nobel prize, which has inevitably 'initiated heated debates about his identity politics' (p. 369). And indeed, Gao's insistence that his work not be defined and limited by national(ist) boundaries seems, as Huang writes, 'to be at odds with Gao's other claims about the role his stage works can play in transforming Chinese theatre' (p. 366).

As will already be evident, a proportion of the work discussed in this book concerns refugees and their stories. The formalised status of 'refugee' accounts for only a proportion of people informally labelled 'exiles'. In many cases, those deemed to be in exile are also (like Gao) citizens of their adopted country, not to mention uniquely or highly skilled individuals – after all, the template we get from ancient Athens and Rome is one where it is 'luminaries' and 'nobles' who suffered exile (Robert Gorman, 'Poets, Playwrights and the Politics of Exile and Asylum in Ancient Greece and Rome', 1994, p. 403). A political status designated under the 1951 UN Refugee Convention, a refugee is one found to have a 'well-founded fear of being persecuted for reasons of race, religion, nationality, membership of a particular social group or political opinion' (article 1). (It should go without saying that the number of people living in such fear, including asylum seekers and internally displaced populations who haven't crossed a political border, greatly exceeds the number formally designated as refugees.) In his 2010 essay 'Refugeeness: What's Good and Not So Good about Being Persecuted and Displaced?', Kim Huynh discusses Albert Einstein, Primo Levi, Leo Strauss and Roman Polanski, as well as his own Vietnamese Australian refugee parents, in order to theorise two interlocking aspects of refugeeness. One is the 'seismic outlook': '[r]efugees are attuned to the fragility of the social structures upon which they stand. They know that whatever is fixed today can be torn away tomorrow. With their ears close to the ground and eyes fixed on the horizon, they are highly sensitive to imminent threats and possibilities' (p. 54). Huynh identifies certain advantages to this outlook: 'for some people, banishment and isolation offers the prospect of personal liberation and growth … fixation on the familiar carries with it the risk of spiritual and intellectual stagnation – a home too easily becomes a prison' (p. 54). This has something in common with Meerzon's investigation of exile as creative liberation. The twin of the seismic refugee outlook, the 'phobic', Huynh observes, 'entails a deep distrust towards others and a stark pessimism about the prospects of human progress' (p. 55).

In *The Politics of Cultural Practice* (2000), Rustom Bharucha expresses suspicion of what he calls the 'privileging of migrancy' and associated ideas about cultural hybridity by some academics and writers (he specifically mentions Homi Bhabha and Salman Rushdie). As someone who 'migrated back' to India after a decade in the United States, Bharucha calls for evaluation of 'those individuals and communities that resist migrancy on the basis of other loyalties and bonds to family, tradition, community, language, and religion that are not always translatable within the norms of liberal individualism' (p. 7). For Bharucha, there is a very real risk that in identifying possibilities for empowerment in migrant experiences, we may 'deny the different historicities of migrancy for which there may be – at times, for some people – nothing to celebrate' (p. 7). It is important to acknowledge that those migrants for whom there is nothing to celebrate are probably less likely to make (or to have the means to make) theatre.

Audiences

The way an audience member interprets and responds to any piece of theatre is influenced by the way he or she imagines his or her relationship to the artists that made the work, and to the story being told. In theatre of migration, this may be summed up, crudely, as: 'Is it by/about *them* or is it by/about *us*?' (though in practice, affiliations are rarely so straightforward). An audience may mostly comprise people for whom the representation of migration is a story of others or otherness, or it may mostly comprise people who perceive the work as about their own community.

The latter conditions are not the dominant ones under which theatre of migration takes place: more often, it is necessarily produced within and across a series of gaps. The politics of position that I referred to earlier applies to audiences just as much as to artists. Artist and audience relationships instantiate the wider structural imbalances of power and status between migrants and those who enjoy the economic, historico-legal, social and linguistic benefits of being 'at home'. As such, theatre of migration is at its most basic level implicated with, and troubled by, power relations within the broader society.

To illustrate this, I want to return to the Greeks. Peter Sellars's American Repertory Theater production of *The Children of Herakles* (Ruhrtriennale, Bottrop, 2002) was an ambitious, multi-platform initiative that sought to democratise conversations across cultural and economic gaps, while harnessing an ancient Greek tragedy as a template for refugee politics. It travelled to Paris and Rome before its three-week run in early 2003 at the ART's base in Cambridge, Massachusetts. The work was split into two parts. In the first, a panel discussion with a rotating group of scholars, policy makers, humanitarian workers and refugees was followed by a performance of Euripides' drama, with cast members speaking into microphones, reminiscent of tribunal-style verbatim theatre. In the second part, food and drink (catered in the Cambridge season by a migrant-owned outlet) was served and audience members were invited to watch a film about refugees.

While it isn't a widely familiar mythic narrative like *The Odyssey* or the *Ramayana*, *The Children of Herakles* represents a pretty close equivalent to what we understand seeking asylum to mean today. Robert Gorman contends that the direct appeals to protection from the people of Athens that appear in Euripides' *The Children of Herakles* and *Medea* and in Sophocles' *Oedipus at Colonus* would in their own time have chimed with prevailing political, moral and religious philosophies: 'Athens had a proud tradition of asylum. By reenacting such scenes before Athenian audiences, Sophocles and Euripides no doubt intended to portray this aspect of their political culture in praiseworthy terms' ('Poets, Playwrights and the Politics of Exile', p. 414).

This view of a theatre culture that reflects (or perhaps activates) certain core values within the polis is obviously complicated in a global era when artists, audiences and entire productions may have undergone transcontinental journeys. The speaking cast of Sellars's twenty-first-century production was multi-ethnic and multi-national. The eponymous children were represented by refugee and immigrant youth, non-speaking cohorts who sat, impassively, on a raised platform. On a couple of occasions the young people went out into the audience to shake hands with spectators, but for the most part, the audience had to absorb the mere fact of their presence; reviewer Scott T. Cummings wrote of a Cambridge, MA performance, '[t]hey just sit there, making no pretense, not even of interest, and every time I look at them their lack of engagement shatters the sham of theatrical illusion, as minimal as it is here. Who are they? Are they having fun? Are they getting paid? What will they buy?' For Cummings, this shattering of illusion was a continual, powerful reminder that the event was a 'civic process' ('Real Children and Other Quandaries', 2003). This doesn't sound so far removed from Gorman's take on Athenian audiences in the fifth century BCE.

With its multiple modalities (discussion, text-based performance, sharing of food and drink, screening), *The Children of Herakles* opened up a range of opportunities for its audiences to engage, participate and respond. Sellars took something that is always the case with live performance – its unrepeatability – and amplified it: very definitely, no two nights were the same, and in this way, the work didn't presume to frame or encapsulate refugee politics. As far as audience experiences were concerned, the instructional, dialogic form of *The Children of Herakles* didn't always hit its targets; in reviewer Don Shewey's view (writing about a performance in Cambridge, MA), 'the pre-play panel stultified the audience with platitudes and propaganda that patronizingly pegged refugees as nothing more than helpless victims. Sellars's "hey-cool-Euripides-watched-CNN" staging of the play kept the audience busy making reductive equations that served neither Euripides nor our understanding of what's at stake for refugees' ('Peter Sellars's CNN Euripides', 2003). On the other hand, academic Kermit Dunkelberg argued (again, of a Cambridge performance) that *The Children of Herakles* 'achieved the potential of theatre to serve (as Sellars termed it in the program) as one of "the last remaining public spaces" in contemporary society' ('*Children of Herakles*', 2003, p. 538). This view of theatre audiences as constituting a forum positions them as active collaborators, rather than as recipients of meaning.

Dunkelberg also describes a 'rich *frisson*' that was generated in the meeting space between ancient myth and contemporary politics (p. 538). The description is telling. In the context of audiences and emotions, myth (and mythopoetics) throws a unique spanner in the works, as Margherita Laera highlights in her account, in the essay 'Reaching Athens' (2011), of her experience as an audience member at *Prometheus in Athens* (Odeon of Herodes Atticus, Athens, 2010), a one-off work by Berlin collective Rimini Protokoll, loosely based on Aeschylus' *Prometheus Bound*. Concerning her own experience as someone who flew in from London specifically to see the work, Laera reflects, '[w]hy does this performance affect me so deeply? I know nobody here, but I do feel some sense of kinship with the people on stage and their half-mythical, half-historical past' (p. 48). Perceiving a unified audience response in repeated 'spontaneous demonstration[s] of warmth' (p. 47), she asks how much 'the "classical" myth, the ancient open-air amphitheatre and the fully lit Parthenon shining behind our backs, have the power to convey a sense of identity, participation and community' (p. 48).

Prometheus in Athens's cast of 103 non-professionals was a demographically representative mass of adults, children and infants, the able-bodied and the disabled, citizens, lawful immigrants and the undocumented. At the start of the performance, each performer came forward to state which character from the Prometheus tragedy they identified with, while their face was projected on a large screen. The work literally posed questions (to which participants answered corporeally in the negative or affirmative by placing themselves in different areas of the vast stage) on topics such as the current economic crisis and concepts such as freedom. As Marissia Fragkou observes in her discussion of the performance in the context of ethics and the enactment of citizenship, *Prometheus in Athens* actualised 'a public space for negotiating the meanings and frames in which citizenship, action, ethics and democracy operate' ('"Other" Stories', 2011, p. 373).

I noted at the start of this book Jean-Luc Nancy's notion that '[m]yth is always the myth of community ... it is always the myth of a communion' (*The Inoperative Community*,

p. 51). This understanding of the way myth works within society elucidates for Laera her own feelings of group identification during *Prometheus in Athens*; she observes that in Nancy's account, 'the storyteller's recounting of myth, which is always a myth of "origin", allows narratives of common belonging to hail the spectators as subjects and as members of a social entity. The performance of myth is, therefore, what enables a community of identifications to emerge' ('Reaching Athens', p. 49). A view of myths as narratives of origin can be broadened to mean *originary* narratives, those that spring from what might be called the pre-cultural, universal, archetypal or genetic. Understood in this capacity, myth has the power to (temporarily) transform 'them' into 'us' and 'us' into 'them'. When 'they' include people living precariously under the shadow of deportation or detention, or more generally of marginalisation and xenophobia, such transformative effects need to be carefully weighed. How many among Sellars's groups of refugee and immigrant youth felt a 'rich *frisson*' as they sat as children of the divine Herakles?

The migrant nation

'Captured outside'

Every day before sunset at the Wagah border crossing on the Grand Trunk Road between Amritsar and Lahore, soldiers of the Indian Border Security Force and the Pakistan Rangers perform a bombastic display of precision goose steps and military salutes, culminating in the simultaneous closing of gates and lowering of flags on both sides. While the event attracts international tourists, it is local spectators who produce roars of patriotic response from rows of tiered seating to nationalist calls over megaphones. Ironically, this controlled display of hostility is a consistent and functioning element of India and Pakistan's notoriously difficult relationship.

The partition of India under the 1947 Mountbatten Plan and the creation of the Islamic nation of Pakistan and an independent India resulted in the uprooting of some 12–14 million people. The violence of these massive population 'exchanges' is woven into the simmering religio-nationalist aggression of the Wagah border ceremony. The kind of attachment to nation symbolised by the ceremony can be accounted for via Benedict Anderson's widely cited formulation of the nation in his book *Imagined Communities* (1991): 'regardless of the actual inequality and exploitation that may prevail in each, the nation is always conceived as a deep, horizontal comradeship. Ultimately it is this fraternity that makes it possible, over the past two centuries, for so many millions of people, not so much to kill, as willingly to die for such limited imaginings' (p. 7).

The trauma of partition and its aftermath reverberates in the nations to which Indian and Pakistani (and later Bangladeshi) people have migrated, chief among which is Britain. Rukhsana Ahmad's *River on Fire* (Lyric Hammersmith, London, 2000), produced by British Asian women's theatre company Kali Theatre, used Sophocles' *Antigone* as a template for engaging with themes of religious antipathy. The play is set against the riots and bombings of late 1992 and early 1993 that erupted in Ayodhya, then in

Pakistan and Bangladesh, and finally in Bombay (as it was then officially known) after the destruction by Hindu nationalists of the Babri mosque in Ayodhya. Also produced by Kali but more explicitly connected with partition was Sonali Bhattacharyya's *A Thin Red Line* (Ulfah Arts, Birmingham, 2007). This co-production by the Birmingham Repertory Theatre and Black Country Touring – oriented around the questions 'Does partition exist in Britain now? If so, have others partitioned us or do we divide ourselves?' – was developed out of community workshops in Birmingham and the Black Country and was presented in community venues before transferring to London's Soho Theatre. While the Wagah border ritual reinforces the political delineation that came into effect in 1947, *River on Fire* and *A Thin Red Line* attempted to ameliorate the social and psychological effects of partition some four thousand miles from where it was enacted.

Categories of migrant are often, when it comes down to it, attempts to claim certain relationships with a nation. The white majorities in nations founded by settler colonialism and convict transportation no longer identify with 'motherlands' in Europe. In contrast, the diasporic subject is conventionally thought of as continuing their identification with a homeland, even among second or third generations. In *On Not Speaking Chinese: Living between Asia and the West* (2001), Ien Ang argues that 'diaspora is a concept of sameness-in-dispersal, not of togetherness-in-difference' (p. 13). Take the way the Greek and Italian diasporas are identified in Australia (especially Melbourne), or the Chinese diaspora in the United States (especially San Francisco and New York), or the Turkish diaspora in Germany (especially Berlin). At the same time, contemporary diasporic conditions of manifold or shifting allegiance mean that, as Robin Cohen writes in *Global Diasporas*, there may be 'no longer any stability in the points of origin, no finality in the points of destination and no necessary coincidence between social and national identities' (p. 174). Whether what Cohen is describing is the freedom of itinerancy or the anxiety of displacement (or statelessness) matters: these shouldn't be crammed into one brave new category of fluidity.

The nation as the sovereign entity it is today may be a recent construction, yoked to the economic and political conditions of modernity, but the idea that underlies it is nothing new: a community to which people are attached, usually for life, and usually as a consequence of birth. Attachment derives from things in common – ethnicity, language, history, mythology, religion, cultural and social traditions, values, institutions, laws – many of which can be adopted, with varying degrees of enthusiasm and success, by the migrant. The most obvious thing that cannot be adopted is ethnicity. An ethnic basis for national belonging can become established even in the absence of a long history of occupation: Ang identifies the persistent fear of invasion from the Asian north as an affective key to the 'psycho-geography' of Australian nationhood (pp. 129–30). I shall return to that shortly.

The Wagah ceremony and various psycho-geographies of invasion attest to the fact that the emotional force of the nation manifests in part as sentiments about *what lies out-side it*. Architectures of exclusion reach a certain level of sophistication in the industrial nation. Giorgio Agamben's writings on sovereign power are particularly useful for understanding a relationship between collective identification and exclusion. He traces the mechanism by which extrajudicial imprisonment (the most relevant example of such a situation, for my purposes, is the immigration detention centre) paradoxically constructs a simultaneous inclusion and exclusion: 'the camp is a piece of territory that is placed outside the normal juridical order; for all that however, it is not simply an external space. According to the etymological meaning of the term *exception* (*ex-capere*), what is being excluded in the camp is *captured outside*, that is, it is included by virtue of its very exclusion' (*Means with-out End*, 2000, p. 40). Our feelings about what our nation is are just as important as our feelings about what it is not. Migration threatens to mess with this, which is one reason zones of exclusion are so tightly controlled by nations that have the means to *capture outside*.

The myth of autochthonous origins

The focus of the rest of this section is on the settler colonial nations of Australia and New Zealand, where although almost everyone is descended relatively recently (in the scheme of things) from migrants, the term 'migrant' is reserved for newer newcomers – post-World War Two, at the very least. The passage of time and intensive mythologising are responsible for this. In his pugnacious three-part essay 'The Foundations of Culture in Australia: An Essay towards National Self-Respect' (1936), the nationalist writer and activist P. R. Stephensen declared:

> Culture in Australia, if it ever develops indigenously, begins not from the Aborigines, who have been suppressed and exterminated, but from British culture, brought hither by Englishmen, Irishmen, and Scotsmen throughout the Nineteenth Century. In a new and quite different environment from that of those damp British Islands we are here developing the culture which evolved there. We spring fully armed from the head of Jove, or fully cultured from the head of John Bull. (p. 3)

Such was his rallying call for cultural autochthony (indigeneity) in Australia, 'the only whiteman's continent' (p. 49).

In 'Towards an Ethics of Location' (2008), Rob Garbutt observes with reference to Australia that a myth of 'autochthonous origins' among the Anglo-Celtic settler-descended population serves several purposes:

> First, the inequalities and violence that accompany the foundation of the state are forgotten through a single unifying myth. ... National origins in forced transportation, exile and migration give way to a story of putting down roots and settling in. Second, autochthony eliminates

> the question: 'To whom does, or did, the land belong?' ... Third, the status of autochthon automatically marks the citizen from the resident non-citizen and foreigner. (p. 185)

To the last part, I would add that inasmuch as the myth of autochthony has been cultivated most successfully among white Australians, it marks certain citizens from other (non-white) citizens. In Australia, as in New Zealand, these dominant groups of citizens have established themselves as 'locals', as the invisible norm.

But not as neatly as Stephensen would have liked. The myth of autochthony has neither cured postcolonial anxieties over the legitimacy of white settlement nor silenced indigenous people (indigenous in the sense of First Nations, not as in Stephensen's appropriation). Theatre in Australia and New Zealand is concerned with negotiating indigenous and non-indigenous relationships as much as citizen and new migrant relationships. What's more, the myth of autochthony isn't the only one with purchase: in 'I Still Call Australia Home: Indigenous Belonging and Place in a White Postcolonizing Society' (2003), Aileen Moreton-Robinson observes that white Australian culture continues to trade on myths of heroic migrancy, 'mobiliz[ing] the legend of the pioneer, "the battler", in its self-legitimization' (p. 23). What we have, then, is a paradoxical meshing of settler mythologies, whereby the *migrant* is somehow also *native*. Indeed, this looks awfully like an example of the decoupling of words that Sara Ahmed, in *Strange Encounters* (p. 79), invites us to consider: the migrant who is not a stranger. In New Zealand, there is a name for this particular position: 'pakeha'.

Upon the federation of its states and territories in 1901, Australia enacted legislation that both effaced its indigenous population and pre-empted immigration by those deemed disruptive to a monocultural project. According to the 1901 constitution, Aboriginal people were to be excluded from census calculations, while under the *Immigration Restriction Act 1901* (popularly known as the White Australia Policy), non-Europeans were prevented from immigrating to Australia via a dictation test. Australia's shift in the latter half of the twentieth century from a 'whiteman's continent' to a 'multicultural' one required some extensive re-narrating at the level of state and federal policy pronouncements. Ahmed argues that official Australian multicultural discourse in the 1980s and 1990s sought to 'reinvent "the nation" over the bodies of strangers' (p. 95), and in doing so contained difference by framing the nation as an underpinning constant: '[t]he notion that any-body can be a real Australian is extremely powerful: it imagines a neutral national space ... open to all; it *sees no difference*' (p. 96).

That's not to say that migration as a trope emerged in Australian theatre only in response to post-White Australia Policy demographic shifts. One of the primary motivations for migration within the vast, colonised continent has traditionally been seasonal work in the agriculture and natural resources sectors, and one of Australia's most lauded plays, Ray Lawler's *Summer of the Seventeenth Doll*

(Union Theatre, Melbourne, 1955), uses this peripatetic economic rhythm as the impetus of its dramatic conflict. Lawler's realist domestic drama represents a landmark in Australian theatre, a turning point akin to that for British theatre of John Osborne's *Look Back in Anger*, which opened at London's Royal Court the following year. Lawler's characters speak in a working-class vernacular, and their world simmers with economic and domestic frustrations amid the oppressive heat of mid-summer. Strikingly, the play portrays (with no discernible moral commentary) unconventional sexual relationships marked by self-reliance, hedonism and ambiguous non-marital obligations. The centrality of seasonal migration to its characters' lives and relationships is not as frequently remarked upon in discussions of the play as it probably should be. The play is set in the seventeenth year in which its two male protagonists, Queensland sugar cane cutters Barney and Roo, have travelled south to spend the summer lay-off in Melbourne with their long-term girlfriends, Olive and Pearl. The slow-burn tragedy of *The Doll*, as it is known in Australia, derives from the predictable intermittency of backbreaking seasonal labour, and the equally predictable inevitability of time and youth passing within and across this cycle. Lawler's is a unique portrait of lives bound together across more than a thousand miles, in the context of new social realities marked by male and female independence, economic uncertainty and, most of all, geographical rootlessness.

Migration within the continent of Australia is central to Jack Davis's *No Sugar* (Festival of Perth, 1985), one of the first full-length plays written in a Western theatrical mode by an Aboriginal Australian writer. But here, internal migration is forced. Set in the late 1920s and early 1930s in the territorially proscribed, racist society of Davis's own childhood, *No Sugar* is among the most important Aboriginal dramas to depict dispossession and the erosion of indigenous traditions as a result of oppressive colonial bureaucracy. In the play, the Munday and Millimurra families are subjected to forced removal from the Government Well Aboriginal Reserve near Northam, Western Australia and relocated to a site determined by the state government. This tactic of geographical siege was used across the continent to sever people from land, adults from self-reliance, children from parents. Like the well-known Australian film *Rabbit Proof Fence* (dir. Phillip Noyce, 2002), Davis's *No Sugar* deploys the figure of the Aboriginal runaway or escapee as enacting crucial resistance in the face of spatial separation.

More recently, the work of Australian playwright Noëlle Janaczewska confronts what multiculturalism might mean in spheres of personal relations and the law, and the dangers of factional antagonisms across migrant communities. Set in Sydney, her play *Songket* (Sydney Opera House Studio, 2003) centres around the relationship between an Australian-born woman of part-Laotian descent and a Hmong Laotian immigrant, socially isolated and barely able to speak English despite his many years in Australia. The relationship, perceived by her as friendship and by him as romantic courtship, ends in an alleged rape. Janaczewska doesn't represent the incident itself, only contrasting accounts of it. The defendant's lawyer enlists the help of his ex, an Australian academic expert in Laotian culture, who becomes increasingly uncomfortable with the way her anthropological knowledge is framed in court. The most challenging thing about *Songket* is the way it interrogates the view that Australian law – with its ally, academic expertise – is a neutral system (neutral in the very same way official multiculturalism says the nation is) into which different cultures are siphoned and ordered. Audiences and readers of the play are prompted to consider whether they agree that as the *law of the land* Australian law is autochthonous in origin, in much the same way as the white Australian citizen. If history troubles the latter mythology, does this mean that Australian rape laws are also contingent?

Janaczewska's play *This Territory* (Sydney Opera House Studio, 2007) lays bare the extent to which cross-cultural and cross-racial tension can be mapped quite literally on to place. The play is in many ways a response to the rise of xenophobia against people of Middle Eastern backgrounds, which in Australia (as in Europe and the United States) has become more prominent since 9/11. *This Territory* was produced by the Australian Theatre for Young People (ATYP) in association with the Powerhouse Youth Theatre. Its youth orientation was purposeful: the play was developed in the wake of the Cronulla race riots of December 2005, which began as a loosely coordinated convergence of white Australians (predominantly local youths) intent on 'reclaiming the beach', south Sydney's Cronulla, after an assault on a group of surf lifesavers by young men of Lebanese origins.

The mob violence and retaliations that followed were unprecedented in scale; international news media reported disturbing images of young Anglo-Celtic Australians defiantly brandishing the national flag, with slogans such as 'ethnic cleansing unit' and 'we grew here, you flew here' – an iteration of the myth of autochthonous origins if ever there was one – scrawled on banners and bare chests.

This Territory was shaped by a six-month research and consultation exercise with young people from across Sydney. It opens with myth: the 'Voices of the Dust' (described as 'our hosts; bizarre cabaret act of songs, myth and social commentary') tell in a Prologue of 'remote days' when 'everyone spoke the same language' (Janaczewska, *Songket and This Territory*, 2003, p. 73). This uncorrupted time and place is named as ancient Mesopotamia, where the god Enki one day 'changed the words in people's mouths' (p. 73), introducing different languages, and thereby division. The play presents a series of confusing and contradictory dialogues, many of them racially barbed, setting out different versions of a violent incident concerning which the young characters are awaiting some kind of judgement. With production notes informing us, '*This Territory* takes place inside a nightmarish beachside RSL club whose décor displays a Mesopotamian theme' (p. 71), and the Voices of the Dust's final characterisation of 'UnAustralia' as '[a] mythic place beyond the pale' (p. 109), comprising those excluded from imagined national community, *This Territory* presents an ambivalent, refracted parody of ancient myth at the same time as it positions myth as a source of wisdom.

New Zealand's founding document, the 1840 Treaty of Waitangi between Maori tribes and the British Crown, while not without deep contention regarding broken promises and translation disputes (crucially, whether 'sovereignty' was ever ceded in the Maori text – as I'll show, this has far-reaching implications), has not required anything near as much red-faced back-pedalling as Australia's *Immigration Restriction Act* of 1901. What the Treaty of Waitangi has meant is that New Zealand has developed a national identity as well as policies responsive to its official biculturalism and bilingualism (not to mention paid financial reparations to Maori via the Waitangi Tribunal). If New Zealand is imagined as two peoples within one nation, its newer migrants, especially non-Europeans, cannot situate themselves as kin of either signatory party to the Treaty.

Renee Liang's play *The Bone Feeder* (Auckland Performing Arts Centre, 2011) recuperates a history of early Chinese presence in New Zealand and in doing so imagines Chinese New Zealand identity that, while not invested with myths of autochthony, is nevertheless literally embedded in the land. Lauren Jackson's production of the magical realist text incorporated acrobatics, martial arts, puppetry and dance, with live music played on Chinese and Maori instruments. The work is based on the 1902 sinking off New Zealand's Hokianga Heads of the *SS Ventnor*, a ship that had been chartered to repatriate the remains of 499 Chinese miners, most from the Otago goldfields. The miners only ever considered themselves temporary residents, but when some of the remains washed up and were retrieved by local Te Roroa and Te Rarawa Maori, who buried them in their urupa (burial sites), they became inextricably connected to New Zealand. Liang folds this evocative story with the character of a fifth-generation Chinese New Zealander who visits the Hokianga in search of his family history. *The Bone Feeder* elucidates contemporary Chinese New Zealand identity as a tension between longing for nostos and connectedness to – and within – the adopted land.

Asylum seekers, refugees and borderlines

If official multiculturalism (and to a lesser extent, biculturalism) contains a nation's others within, a political border is the near-totemic site of inoculation from (unwanted) others *outside* the nation. As a basic consequence of its geography (with outlying islands close enough to Indonesia to be reached by rickety people-smuggling vessels) Australia has, unlike its isolated neighbour New Zealand, had the opportunity over the past decade or more to build an edifice of increasingly heated political and cultural discourse about unauthorised asylum seekers (specifically 'boatpeople'; those who seek asylum in Australia via the orderly means of an aeroplane, not to mention the substantial annual humanitarian intake, aren't subject to anywhere near the same intensity of debate and don't ignite the imaginations of the populace in the same way).

In 1992, Australia implemented a mandatory detention policy for all unauthorised asylum seekers. In the years since, this policy has been modified (and during a brief window in 2008, was to be abandoned), but it is currently bipartisan and seemingly entrenched, with detention facilities on the mainland and offshore. The latter include the Australian territory of Christmas Island, as well as recently reopened centres on the South Pacific island nation of Nauru and on Manus Island, Papua New Guinea. Australia has also gradually extended its notorious 2001 legislation that excised island territories from its migration zone, to the point where the *Migration Amendment (Unauthorised Maritime Arrivals and Other Measures) Act 2013* excised the entire continent of Australia from the migration zone. Excision does not affect Australia's large Exclusive Economic Zone, where it holds special rights over exploration and marine resources, or the rights of Australian citizens and visa holders to travel within and across excised places. But most asylum seekers intercepted in what's called an 'excised offshore place' never legally 'arrive' in Australia at all, in the sense that they are excluded from applying directly for Australian protection visas. This is precisely what Homi Bhabha is describing when he writes about cultures of surveillance that, as I quoted in the first section, separate 'the good migrant from the bad migrant' (*The Location of Culture*, p. xvii).

Over the past decade, theatre and performance in Australia have been a relatively conspicuous part of the national conversation about asylum seekers, and in particular, a voice of opposition to the most punitive discourse and policy. Following their respective releases from immigration detention, Shahin Shafaei and Towfiq Al-Qady wrote and performed solo plays that sought to communicate something of their experiences to Australian audiences.

An Iranian playwright and director, Shafaei toured his *Refugitive* (New Mercury Theatre, Sydney, 2002) to more than forty metropolitan and rural locations across Australia between 2002 and 2004. The work centred on an unnamed man undertaking a hunger strike in an Australian detention centre. But rather than offer a tragic narrative, Shafaei incorporated satire and slapstick that engaged with Western popular culture (such as references to Russell Crowe and to Homer Simpson's repeated strangulation of his son Bart). Shafaei's performances were followed by question-and-answer sessions that often went on for longer than the fifty-minute show. Iraqi painter and writer Al-Qady's solo play, *Nothing but Nothing* (Metro Arts Theatre, Brisbane, 2006), complicated the typical model of testimony as witnessing to one's direct experience: his poetic narrative spoke for the communities (family, friends, fellow Iraqis) impacted by trauma via a shifting subjectivity that appropriated the memories (and literally, the first-person voices) of others. Shafaei's and Al-Qady's performances collapsed the usual gap between refugees and their theatrical representation, requesting that audiences regard them face to face as new co-members of a national community.

Shafaei and Al-Qady are fairly unique, their solo works written and produced with significant amounts of creative autonomy. More often, asylum seeker and refugee theatre in Australia involves collaborations between Australians and refugees, or in some cases, asylum seekers still in detention. Verbatim theatre has emerged (as in Britain and the United States) as a dominant form whereby Australian actors serve as proxies for asylum seekers, speaking their words, transcribed and arranged into a performance text. Nigel Jamieson's *In Our Name* (Belvoir St Theatre, Sydney, 2002), which used material from interviews with an Iraqi family held for more than three years in different Australian detention centres before being deported, and Don Mamouney's *Citizen X* (Sidetrack Theatre, Sydney, 2002), devised from the letters of detained asylum seekers, are just two examples.

As well as the obvious functions of 'giving voice to' or 'speaking for' asylum seekers and refugees, theatre and performance that engage with contentious asylum politics can serve the interests of citizens, inasmuch as they demarcate an alternative imagined community. James Goodman observes that Australia's asylum seeker solidarity movements are bifurcated, one 'geared to national policy change, effectively to remaking "the nation", and reclaiming national pride against the shame of refugee detention', and the other more expansive in expressing 'anger and outrage in the name of human empathy and dignity' ('Refugee Solidarity', 2009, pp. 270–71). Both, he maintains, are underpinned by deep emotional responses to asylum seekers: '[t]he aim here is to evoke an emotional response to an issue, one that elicits cognitive reflection and action. This involves the mobilization of moral emotions' (p. 272). The mobilisation of moral emotions can be a visceral act. Performance artist Mike Parr's gruesome durational piece *Close the Concentration Camps* (Monash University Museum of Art, Melbourne, 2002) saw Parr sitting on a chair for five hours with his ears, eyes and mouth sewn up and his trouser leg ripped open at the thigh, where the word 'alien' was branded. Between 2002 and 2004 other acts of bodily investment included solidarity fasts performed in public spaces by well-known Australians. These took place during a period when media reports of asylum seekers' self-injuries and hunger strikes in detention centres were prominent. Such use of bodies in pain communicates the citizen's ethical responsibility for people detained extrajudicially by the state. That these protesting bodies have been unable to act as bargaining tools for substantial change in policy doesn't diminish their commitment, but it does raise the question of whether such actions can serve asylum seekers as comprehensively as they serve alternative visions of Australian national identity.

Leveraging indigenous belonging

Indigenous people in postcolonial nations are caught within European taxonomic systems. Just as the word 'antipodes' presupposes Europe as a geographical starting point, the classifications 'Aboriginal' or 'native' can only come into existence *with reference to* or *measured against* those who came (and conquered) later. Some words betray oppressive epistemologies more blatantly than others – compare, for instance, 'Maori' (which means 'normal' or 'natural') to 'American Indian' (famously, Columbus's mistake).

Indigeneity now circulates as a commodity in statecraft, having become a desirable component of postcolonial narratives of nationhood. In New Zealand and, latterly, Australia, indigenous performance has been valued as a unique element of national performance: Maori Powhiri (welcome) and Aboriginal Australian Welcome to Country ceremonies are now fixtures of official events such the opening of Parliament. While essentialist understandings of indigeneity will always be reductive, it may be said that self-defined Aboriginal Australian identity and Maori identity (both of which are ethnic, cultural and political amalgamations) are *strategically* essentialist, characterised by ancestral or genealogical conceptions of community and affiliation, an interest in cultural and ecological custodianship and, in some cases, the assertion of unextinguished sovereignty.

This last component remembers the conditions of the nation's founding and radically questions its legitimacy. One of the key sites for such questioning is over the bodies of newcomers: the welcoming or rejection of migrants. In recent years, performative strategies by indigenous activists in Australia and New Zealand have reoriented that modern-day amulet, the passport. In doing so, they've homed in on the rationalisation of identity that I cited in the first section of the book as crucial to the way strangers and locals are designated. In October 2009, Australian Prime Minister Kevin Rudd telephoned the Indonesian president, Susilo Bambang Yudhoyono, to request that a boat carrying Sri Lankan Tamils, heading for Australia's Christmas Island, be intercepted and escorted to the port of Merak, on the northwestern tip of Java. Indonesia obliged, but a six-month-long standoff ensued when the asylum seekers refused to disembark until they had been assured passage to Australia. At a refugee support rally in Melbourne on 1 May 2010,

Aboriginal Australian activists responded to the standoff by producing Original Nation Passports for the Merak asylum seekers. Leader Robbie Thorpe, flanked by other activists publicly signing stacks of passports outside Melbourne's Trades Hall, announced: 'we want to make it clear that the Aboriginal people, the true sovereigns of this land, are offering them a passport to enter into our territorial waters, and our land', adding, 'we're the colonised refugees'.

In New Zealand, similar sentiments about indigenous sovereignty and oppression-in-common are interwoven with ideas about regional kinship, with Polynesian ethnicity a pretext for Maori activism in support of Pacific overstayers facing deportation. Pacific Islanders are among the poorest communities in New Zealand, but their impact on the nation's artistic landscape is considerable, celebrated most visibly in the annual Pasifika Festival in Auckland, home to the world's largest Pacific population. If not for the exclusive agreement drawn up with the British in 1840, Pacific peoples might, arguably, have a claim to belonging in New Zealand second only to that of Maori. In June 2009, New Zealand police charged Maori activist Gerrard Otimi with deception causing loss and giving immigration advice without a licence after he sold visas to around 100 Pacific (mainly Samoan) immigrants desperate to remain in New Zealand after the expiry of their work visas. Otimi charged 500 New Zealand dollars per visa, which consisted of a certificate and passport sticker stating that the holder was a whangaied (adopted) member of Otimi's hapu (sub-tribal grouping) and had the right to remain.

Unlike the production of Original Nation Passports by Thorpe and his colleagues, Otimi's activism – because his hapu visa is, whatever else it might be, a statement of Maori sovereignty – constitutes a financial as well as political transaction: Otimi made a nice sum of money from the enterprise. His appropriation of the visa and passport as objects of political power includes an appropriation of the capitalist economics imbricated in this power. Anyone who has applied for a passport or visa will know that the financial costs (to say nothing of the emotional investment) are high – for many, prohibitively so. Documented belonging within the modern nation is held at a premium. Otimi's action provokes the question of what happens when a right to remain granted by a Maori sovereign authority operates according to a similar rubric of value and exchange to a right to remain offered for purchase by a nation's recognised immigration authority. If the status of hapu whangai for the Pacific Islanders formalised their Polynesian kinship with Otimi, it also came, quite literally, at a price.

The issue of Otimi's fraudulence – something we might assess by weighing his knowledge that financial payment would not produce the kind of legal status the Pacific migrants presumably believed (or *wanted to believe*) they were purchasing against his convictions regarding the legal status that Maori sovereignty *should* hold – is complicated and fraught. Otimi's use of his Maori-ness to exert power over vulnerable people, his brazen assertion of right without obligation, disrupts and reorients simplistic lines of association between indigeneity, ethical hospitality and anti-capitalism. Otimi's motives were at least partly financial and exploitative. Nevertheless, his actions demand an appraisal of the ontology of sovereignty – *how* Maori sovereignty may be said to exist and what the consequences of this existence are (for further discussion, see Emma Cox, 'Sovereign Ontologies', 2013).

Lines of connection between marginalised insiders and marginalised outsiders underpinned acclaimed Samoan choreographer Lemi Ponifasio's dance work *Tempest: Without a Body* (Vienna Festival, 2007). The work, which has toured to New Zealand, Australia, various locations in Europe, Canada and the United States, is a dystopian meditation on state biopower and individual liberty that takes Shakespeare's narrative (especially the trope of bodily subjugation) as a point of departure. Its most direct reference to mechanisms of post-9/11 exceptional power was a warrior challenge by high-profile Maori activist Tame Iti, performed against the backdrop of a large projected image of Ahmed Zaoui, an Algerian refugee who was extrajudicially imprisoned in New Zealand after being issued with a Security Risk Certificate in 2003. The juxtaposition was potent. Iti, along with members of his family and other activists, was living in a remote Urewera mountains property that was dramatically and controversially raided in 2007 by New Zealand police, who suspected it was being used for paramilitary training. The alignment of Iti and Zaoui in *Tempest: Without a Body* frames the two men as comparable subjects of punitive anti-terror laws and civil liberty violations. Like Otimi's activism, Iti's performance effectively leverages his indigeneity in the vexed context of 'undesirable' migrants in New Zealand. Both men hold clear convictions about unextinguished Maori sovereignty, and both identified the right to decide which migrants can remain in New Zealand as being at the heart of sovereign power.

The migrant city

Time and tactics

Worldwide, people are migrating to cities at an astonishing rate. Our current period of rapid urbanisation has been described as the greatest movement of people in human history (Doug Saunders, *Arrival City*, 2011, p. 1). This final section of *Theatre & Migration* situates the contemporary global city as the coalface where past, present and *future* meanings of migrant and native identity are (to be) tested and contested. I look at theatre productions, festivals and cross-form collaborations that reveal some of the ways migration is figured – sometimes in the mainstream, sometimes at the margins – as key to questions about history, allegiance and belonging in the city. The three case studies for this discussion are London, Cape Town and Toronto.

I've drawn attention to the ways in which the nation can be the object of shifting and competing ideas about sovereignty, territoriality, indigeneity and affiliation. But set alongside the amorphous, slippery contemporary city, the nation – defined by political powers, immured by borders and fed by the desires of citizens for coherent community – looks comparatively stable. In *Arrival City*, his intricate and exhaustive study of how migrants are reshaping cities around the world, journalist Doug Saunders describes an 'arrival' zone in Dhaka, a slum that is officially outside the city's municipal boundaries and therefore ineligible for infrastructure and schooling provision, but which is destined eventually to become incorporated into the city proper (p. 52). Such malleability – and particularly this process of absorbing the fringes – isn't a feature of national borders. Even when a city becomes a touchstone for a nation's hopes, aspirations and imagined identifications – as London did in 2012 – it is always in flux, always exceeding its own definitions. According to Homi Bhabha in *The Location of Culture*, 'it is to the city that the migrants, the minorities, the diasporic come to change the history of the nation' (pp. 169–70).

Michel de Certeau's theorisation of cities and the 'tactics' of individuals who live in them offers a useful frame for a discussion of migrant practices in city spaces. In his chapter 'Walking in the City' from *The Practice of Everyday Life*, de Certeau contends that the utopian concept and discourse of 'the city' is founded upon three ordering principles: first, 'the production of its *own* space (*un espace propre*): rational organization that must thus repress all the physical, mental and political pollutions that would compromise it'; second, 'the substitution of a nowhen, or of a synchronic system' that flattens 'all the data in a plane projection'; and third, 'the creation of a *universal* and anonymous *subject* which is the city itself', which 'like a proper name, thus provides a way of conceiving and constructing space on the basis of a finite number of stable, isolatable, and interconnected properties' (p. 94). 'Undesirable' migrants are constructed as 'pollutions that would compromise' the ordered city. Even inclusive discourse can betray anxieties over the contaminant such migrants represent: implied in Liberal Democrats leader Nick Clegg's controversial proposal during the 2010 UK election campaign for an 'amnesty' that would put long-term illegal immigrants on the path to tax-paying citizenship was the idea of organising the spaces – most conspicuously, London – where the illegal population is concentrated.

Everyday disruption of organisational strategies, de Certeau argues, takes the form of the 'tactics' of denizens: 'the city is left prey to contradictory movements that counterbalance and combine themselves outside the reach of panoptic power. … Beneath the discourses that ideologize the city, the ruses and combinations of powers that have no readable identity proliferate; … they are impossible to administer' (p. 95). De Certeau's claim that the 'Concept-city is decaying' (p. 95) and being 'outlived' by 'microbe-like' (p. 96) practices is more penetrating than he could have imagined in the 1980s: by invoking the vantage point of the 110th floor of New York's World Trade Center as the exemplar of panoptic, god-like knowledge, de Certeau unwittingly inscribed his own dismantling of the 'nowhen'. Taken together, the theatre and performance discussed in this section belie (by creative rather than destructive practices) the idea that the dynamic migrant cities of London, Cape Town and Toronto could ever be encompassed by the 'timeless' rationale of the 'nowhen'.

London: arrival capital

I began the second section of this book with an account of the Wagah border ceremony, a performance of chest-thumping, militaristic nationalism which is also a tourist spectacle. Just as baffling, in its own way, to outsiders and inspiriting to insiders was the opening ceremony of the London 2012 Olympic Games. In a familiar extrapolation – familiar, that is, to Olympic ceremonies generally, but acute in the British context – the work of branding the capital city merged with that of branding the nation: here, a Britain made great by its industrial revolution, nurtured by its nationalised healthcare and connected to the world via the Internet and communications technologies that it pioneered. The Olympic Park Legacy Company, the consortium that oversaw the Olympics infrastructure, emphasised the Park's general proximity to the East End, a traditional place of arrival for newcomers, and thus conscripted several east London boroughs as beneficiaries of 'redevelopment'. And Danny Boyle's opening ceremony sought to be explicitly multicultural, to proclaim: *London was built by those who were born here and those who have migrated here.*

While the ceremony's material affiliations with neo-liberal and corporate interests are obvious, the ideological affiliations of its creators, and those of its mostly volunteer participants, are much trickier to pin down. This is due to the event's more wayward takes on triumphalism, the most tactical of which was the section performed by health sector workers valorising the National Health Service, a tribute that stood in direct opposition to the Cameron government's facilitation of gradual privatisation (and left several US commentators bemused). Rural to urban and post-war migrations were also part of the ambiguous mix. It wasn't hard to read the ceremony's first few minutes, in which green pastures were swept aside to make way for dark, belching smokestacks, as less a reification of the teleology of progress and more a precipitous overhaul of labour relations (the section was named Pandemonium, John Milton's neologism for the capital of hell). Dizzying lines of performers representing the new urban industrial workforce were followed by the arrival of a ship rendered in newsprint collage, standing for the *MV Empire Windrush*. The performers who portrayed these post-war migrants from the former British West Indies walked soberly into the stadium dressed in suits and flat caps, suitcases in hand, ready to work.

The degree to which different migrant groups can manoeuvre within the frame of a city's endorsed narratives has a lot to do with where they sit on a spectrum from *heritage* to *undesirable*. The opening ceremony's *Windrush* scene communicated that post-war migrants from Britain's former colonies have become part of London's heritage, much like the Huguenot and later Jewish migrant communities that built up in and around the East End from the late seventeenth to the early twentieth centuries. Heritage is closely linked with moral notions of 'contribution', especially to industry but also to cultural and social life. The heritage factor underpins recent collaborations between the National Maritime Museum in Greenwich and London theatre companies Talawa Young People's Theatre (the youth training branch of Talawa, London's principal black British theatre company), Tara Arts (see below) and British East Asian theatre company Yellow Earth, which have produced interactive performances at the museum aimed at young people. These collaborations with a capital-N 'National' venue made it the prerogative of ethnic minority theatre companies to present their own histories, and in the same move positioned slavery (in the case of Talawa), Indian Lascars (Tara) and *Cutty Sark* crewmembers (Yellow Earth) as inheritances of all who inhabit – and contribute to – Britain's arrival capital.

But London theatre started to get to grips with post-war black and Asian migrant cultures and contexts long before these became accepted as part of larger narratives of national identity. In the late 1940s, Robert Adams founded the professional Negro Repertory Arts Theatre. Adams was an immigrant from Guyana who had arrived in London in the mid-1930s and established a successful career as a stage and screen actor. In the immediate post-war period, Adams and other Caribbean immigrant performers also acted at London's Unity Theatre, which grew out of the Workers' Theatre Movement. In 1958, Trinidadian playwright Errol John's *Moon on a Rainbow Shawl*, a play set in Trinidad that explores the hopes and fantasies associated with migrating to Britain, became the Royal Court's first play by a black playwright; it was staged in New York in 1962 and has been revived on numerous occasions since, most recently at the National Theatre in 2012 and by Talawa Theatre in 2014. British South Asian theatre in London has been dominated since the late 1970s by Tara Arts, which has built a substantial archive of original plays as well as adaptations of European texts. The company's most ambitious migration-themed work to date is *Journey to the West* (England tour, 2002), a highly physical, multilingual (or 'Binglish', to use artistic director Jatinder Verma's neologism) trilogy that developed out of earlier works-in-progress, *Exodus* (1998), *Genesis* (1999) and *Revelations* (2000).

London theatres are not in the business solely of minority self-representation when it comes to immigrant narratives concerning Britain, as white British playwright Richard Bean's satire *England People Very Nice* (National Theatre, London, 2009) attested. Directed by Nicholas Hytner, the play imagined successive waves of newcomers to London's East End via loosely connected vignettes set in different eras. The show was metatheatrically bookended by scenes of detained asylum seekers being led in a play-devising project. The detailed programme, with illustrated historical précis of centuries of migration to London, seemed to position the production as something of a historical or pedagogical event in itself. The play sparked controversy – and the tactical disruption of an on-stage protest during a panel discussion – for its perceived racist stereotyping. Its defenders pointed out that every culture and ethnicity was fair game, including white British and Irish.

Anyone with a passing understanding of satire will know that, on their own, over-the-top foreign accents and faux-jocular racial antagonisms (both of which were littered throughout Bean's play) aren't straightforwardly 'offensive'; they need to be situated in terms of intersections of gender and class, on the level both of representation (what stories are being told) and of social practice (who is telling and hearing them). *England People Very Nice* contrasted two central relationships between sexually experienced white women and sexually conservative (but voracious) South Asian men with the comparatively strict mores of Muslim women. The play's overwhelming preponderance of crude, belligerent working-class characters were positioned as a source of hilarity for the National's mostly middle-class, white patrons (take the lines, 'how's a Muslim woman to integrate? You get your arse tattooed, a crack habit, and seven kids by seven dads'). By such accounts, *England People Very Nice* was, quite simply, offensive. But whether it was *inherently* racist (or sexist or classist) or not is perhaps less interesting than the fact that it generated conversations about racism and theatrical representation, with a slew of articles in print and online media. In this capacity it was a lightning rod for assessments of London's multiculturalism, not to mention discussions about how well and for whom satire works in different performance contexts.

A production that, in contrast, undertook more than a caricature of the migrant cultures it portrayed, *Feast* (Young Vic, London, 2013) was a spirited, witty performance of Yoruba histories *and* a challenging evocation of uneasy or unconvivial multiculturalism. Directed by Rufus Norris and written by no less than five playwrights (from four continents) – Yunior García Aguilera, Rotimi Babatunde, Marcos Barbosa, Tanya Barfield and Gbolahan Obisesan – *Feast* traversed a 400-year span of time, imagining some of the scatterings of the global Yoruba diaspora via an episodic narrative structure oriented around the lives of women (themselves manifestations of orishas, or deities).

The consequence of multi-authorship was that several substantial stories were told. A scene set in eighteenth-century rural west Africa, where fears of slavers abound, gave way to a pitiable conversation in a Brazilian farm-house in 1888 where, following emancipation, an elderly slave begs to remain with her former owner (a man whom, decades earlier, she had been made to nurse, relinquishing her own infant). A sit-in at a southern US diner during the era of the African American civil rights movement was movingly presented in dialogue and song by a row of actors sitting on barstools, facing the audience. This was followed by a comic and faintly surreal encounter in a Cuban brothel in 2008 that implied some surprising intersections between white American masculinity and Afro-Cuban women's sexuality, between money and power and between empiricism and superstition. A contemporary gathering of an educated New York family laid out debates over the value of academic research into African American rap. Finally, the spikiest part of *Feast* was set in London in 2012: a heated exchange between a black British female athlete and a black British man who interrupts her on the street with a series of questions about the sexual politics of her relationship with her white male coach. Dramatic scenes were intertwined with song (folk, gospel, hip hop) and movement (from contemporary and Cuban dance to a male strip routine) and overseen by a trickster figure that appeared in various guises, occasionally accompanied by a live chicken. The overall effect of this sprawling, multi-tonal work – which even managed to smuggle in a joke about Nigerian scam emails – was to temper the joyous with the provocative.

The episodic or vignette mode of storytelling appears frequently in theatre of migration. The effect of this device is to build up an aggregate picture of 'types', emphasising commonality over individuality. Such aggregation is conducive to the kind of mythopoetic envisioning of migrants that I discussed in the first section. Vignettes formed the basis of *The Arrival* (England tour, 2013), based on a graphic novel by Shaun Tan and co-produced by London-based companies Tamasha Theatre and Circus Space, in association with human rights outreach organisation Ice and Fire Theatre. Scripted by Sita Brahmachari and directed by Tamasha's artistic director, Kristine Landon-Smith, *The Arrival* used circus and text-based theatre to traverse several non-specified time periods, presenting stories of arrival to London of refugees and immigrants from Nigeria, China, Sudan and Poland. The production's central figure, a character from Nigeria, was costumed almost identically to the '*Windrush* generation' in the London Olympics opening ceremony. Curiously, in a question-and-answer session following opening night at London's Jacksons Lane theatre (the tour's last stop), Brahmachari observed that this character could be read as a post-war migrant, or as a migrant from *any* or *no* time. Landon-Smith offered a similarly mythopoetic perspective on how *The Arrival* engaged with migration by referring in the Q&A to an 'age-old story of migration'. At the same time, testimonies from refugees were interwoven into the production, implying a documentary function that seemed to encourage a certain blurring of actor and character: the very first questioner in the Q&A asked how many of the performers were UK-born.

Cape Town: desegregating space

Cape Town grew out of international migration. The world's first global corporation, the Dutch East India Company, depended on the calm waters of Table Bay as a place for its ships to drop anchor safely away from the often treacherous Cape of Good Hope. A geographical and psychological mid-way point on trade routes between Europe and India (and further east), Cape Town became a key supply station for the Dutch from 1652, and then for the British after the Anglo-Dutch Treaty of 1814. Today, it is the second most populous city in a nation that receives more asylum applications than any other Refugee Convention signatory in the world: according to the UNHCR's 2014 Country Operations Profile, South Africa is host to more than 350,000 asylum seekers and refugees, 70,000 of whom are assisted by the UNHCR (unhcr.org/pages/49e485aa6.html).

Of course, before morphing into a troubled postcolonial melting pot, Cape Town went from imperial trade hub to international pariah under apartheid-era trade embargos and cultural boycotts. With South Africa isolated from the outside world for much of the latter half of the twentieth century, its non-white residents endured successive forced removals, what might be called 'micro' migrations (micro in terms of geographical distance, not population). In Cape Town, the segregationist regime redrew city boundaries: 'native/black', 'coloured' and 'Indian/Asian' populations (many the descendants of slaves and indentured labourers transported by the Dutch and the British from across Africa, Madagascar, Southeast Asia and India) were separated from 'whites' in designated zones. The legislation that facilitated South Africa's forced micro migrations was the *Group Areas Act 1950* and its amendments. John Western, in his study of social geography *Outcast Cape Town* (1996), observes that the Act 'implemented carefully conceived urban plans designed by Whites to maintain White control. In Cape Town it so happened that most of the people in the way of these plans were those racially classified as Coloured' (p. xvi). At the same time as forcing people from their homes, the apartheid regime maintained movement controls that had been in place since the eighteenth century with the creation of ten Bantustans, or black homelands, and the implementation of Pass Laws, which required black Africans ('natives') to carry pass books when outside their designated areas. One of the effects of this was that a large population of (mostly male) migrants were compelled to go to cities and mines for work.

One of the best-known South African plays to deal with this notorious history of population concentration and internal labour migration is Athol Fugard, John Kani and Winston Ntshona's *Sizwe Banzi Is Dead*. The play premiered in 1972 at Cape Town's Space Theatre, a non-segregationist fringe theatre, which the following year staged the first production of *The Island*, another Fugard, Kani and Ntshona collaboration. *Sizwe Banzi Is Dead* dramatises the absurdities of bureaucratised identity and movement restrictions under apartheid via its eponymous protagonist, a black man or Bantu, who steals the pass book of a dead man in order to continue working in Port Elizabeth. Two years after its Cape Town premiere, the play was produced in London and New York. Its post-apartheid performance history includes two recent successful UK productions, one in which Kani and Ntshona performed (National Theatre, 2007) and the other a Young Vic and Eclipse Theatre Company touring co-production (2013 and 2014).

Today, one of Cape Town's major theatres bears the name of Fugard, the white playwright who, along with Kani and Ntshona, was at the forefront of resistance to apartheid. Fugard's plays were rare exceptions to international boycotts of South African cultural exports, being staged during apartheid in theatres from London to Melbourne. The Fugard Theatre stands in the inner city area of District Six, the infamous site of mass demolition of homes from the late 1960s to 1982 and the removal of some 60,000 'coloured' residents. The theatre's development from the mid-2000s is part of efforts over recent years to revitalise as well as memorialise District Six. As Gordon Pirie notes in his 2007 essay 'Reanimating a Comatose Goddess: Reconfiguring Central Cape Town', 'the original campaigning slogan "Hands off District Six" is changing to "Hands on District Six"' (p. 146).

Just as creative industries and some former residents have returned to sites of forced removal, so too have diverse performers started to return to once segregated streets and public zones. The Kaapse Klopse minstrel carnival is re-emerging as a significant annual event in the city. It originated as a celebration of emancipation among Cape Town's Malay slaves and is now dominated by the Cape Malay community, with some involvement by black South Africans. The carnival has run into conflict with city authorities that associate it with gang culture and public disorder in what Mara Kardas-Nelson, in a January 2013 article for South Africa's *Mail and Guardian*, describes as the authorities' 'notoriously combative past with the minstrels'. Quoting the director of social history collections at Iziko Museums of South Africa, Lalou Meltzer, Kardas-Nelson writes:

> Despite years of campaigning, it wasn't until 2012 that the minstrels were allowed to conduct the march along their preferred, historic route from District Six to Bo-Kaap. 'For people who were kicked out of town, to follow that route ... which traces the history of the community and connects working class Cape Town [is] very emotional. It's bittersweet,' explains Meltzer. ('Kaapse Klopse Still March to Their Own Beat')

Kaapse Klopse represents the Cape Malay community's second emancipation: their return to and embodied re-mapping of parts of the city from which they were so recently forcibly erased. Their negotiations with the authorities are a testament to what de Certeau calls the 'surreptitious creativities' that occur within disciplinary organisation of space (*The Practice of Everyday Life*, p. 96).

The post-apartheid migration that provokes even greater antipathy than the return of non-white citizens comes from across South Africa's borders. As Western notes, the repeal of Pass Laws and the installation of democracy accelerated an influx of people from Mozambique, Zimbabwe and elsewhere, many of them asylum seekers and undocumented migrants (*Outcast Cape Town*, pp. xxi–xxii). Attacks against African migrants are frequent, and in May 2008 a wave of xenophobic violence spread across South Africa following evictions in Johannesburg of non-nationals from their homes. One mode of response to such violent assaults on living space is to reimagine the way spaces, especially dense urban areas, may be used and shared. In 2009, Cape Town's public arts festival, Infecting the City (a name wonderfully suggestive of de Certeau's 'microbe-like' tactics), was themed 'Home Affairs', and sought to respond to hostility against foreigners via a range of free performances and art installations in public, communal areas. Several works were collaborative projects made by teams from Europe, South Africa and southern African states that gathered in Cape Town several weeks before the festival began.

Another mode of response to the trauma of xenophobia is autobiography. Writer-performer Jonathan Nkala's play *The Crossing* (Baxter Theatre Centre, Cape Town, 2008) recalls his journey from Kwekwe, Zimbabwe, to Cape

Town. The semi-comic solo work has been presented to student groups and has toured to Durban, Grahamstown, Harare and as far as Albuquerque. In a discussion with Nkala and *The Crossing*'s South African adaptor-director Bo Petersen, Miki Flockemann argues that the play shows 'one of the underlying causes of xenophobia' in South Africa to be vast economic inequality: 'the discrepancy between rich and poor is so great that you have no way of addressing it. So you can't shout at the people who are in control so you target a proxy. ... The foreigner becomes the proxy of that force or that power that you actually want to address' ('Performing Xenophobia', 2009, p. 210). *The Crossing* represents some of the deep-seated anger Nkala has faced, including that of a truck driver who picked him up, only to pull out a gun and unleash a torrent of demeaning insults. Flockemann suggests that Nkala is 'like the mirror of his [the driver's] own rage', a man who is 'like him because he is also black' and yet 'not like him because he's a foreigner' (p. 210).

It is well known that one of the major sources of asylum seekers and undocumented migrants to South Africa in recent years has been Zimbabwe. Shannon Morreira describes the hostile reception that individuals fleeing the dire situation in Zimbabwe have faced in South Africa: '[a]sylum seekers leaving Zimbabwe with ideas of South Africans as "struggle brothers" and with local ideas of how to treat strangers, quickly learned that they were perceived as outsiders and that their notions of regionalism and commonality were disregarded in favour of notions of sovereignty and difference' ('Seeking Solidarity', 2007, p. 434). Nkala's *The Crossing* was in part a response to the surge of violence in 2008, but as he says, xenophobia is a daily reality for him as a Zimbabwean in South Africa; in the above-mentioned discussion Nkala describes being verbally or physically abused in Cape Town 'almost every day' (p. 209).

Cape Town's Magnet Theatre address xenophobia and the plight of asylum seekers in the physical theatre piece *Every Year, Every Day, I Am Walking*. Directed by the theatre's artistic director Mark Fleishman and performed by two women, company co-director Jennie Reznek and company regular Faniswa Yisa, the work presents a story of a mother and daughter's forced displacement following a violent attack on their village and their arduous journey to Cape Town to seek refuge. The work's performance history is itself a continuing travel story: since its premiere in 2006 at the African Festival of Youth and Children's Theatre in Yaoundé, Cameroon, *Every Year, Every Day, I Am Walking* has toured throughout southern Africa, as well as to London and Newcastle; Buenos Aires; Thrissur, Kerala; Belém, São Paulo and Brasilia; Malmö; Stuttgart; Okinawa; and Amherst, Massachusetts.

With its scant language and recurrence of physical tropes to represent the arduous journey (most memorably, the evocative use of shoes as hand-held puppets that variously walk side by side, or trace the curve of a body, or trudge dejectedly through sand and ash), the work produced poetic affects rather than a specific testimonial-style narrative such as that offered by Nkala in *The Crossing*. Mother and daughter's negotiation of Home Affairs bureaucracy in Cape Town (the work's one geographical reference point) is juxtaposed with a fable about African elephants' ancient migratory patterns, severed by fiercely guarded political borders. By not specifying its protagonists' origin or trajectory, only their destination, *Every Year, Every Day, I Am Walking* can transpose itself into different performance settings and resonate differently for different constituencies, many of whom may have experienced violent displacement. According to Yvette Hutchison, Western tendencies, derived from the European Enlightenment, to equate a play's historical veracity (signified primarily by words) with the value of 'truth' don't necessarily make sense for South African theatre or for African philosophy more generally: '[i]n the African context, the story is itself important as a mode through which we can know ourselves and explore our history, identity and collective value systems. It is no less true for being fictional or constructed. At some level it may even suggest greater truth, abstracted beyond the specific' ('Verbatim Theatre in South Africa', 2009, p. 211). In this way, the question of whether Magnet Theatre's production presented a 'true' asylum seeker narrative means different things depending on who is asking.

The abstraction of *Every Year, Every Day, I Am Walking* hasn't always served it well politically outside Africa. As I have discussed in a recent article ('Victimhood, Hope and the Refugee Narrative', 2012), the reception of the work in the different international locations to which it toured revealed marked differences in terms of apparent awareness of tensions in Cape Town, and South Africa generally, surrounding asylum seekers, refugees and undocumented migrants. In London, many reviewers resorted to facile platitudes about struggle and redemption, and made no mention, for instance, of South Africa's spate of xenophobic violence in 2008, something that must surely be etched into the consciousness of Magnet Theatre's local audience members since those horrific events.

Toronto: multicultural configurations

Toronto may be half a world away from Cape Town, but the two cities have in common interlinked histories of European colonisation, the transatlantic slave trade and the displacement and indenturing of indigenous people. A recent theatrical collaboration between Toronto and Cape Town artists explored these links: *Ubuntu (The Cape Town Project)* (Tarragon Theatre, Toronto and Neptune Theatre, Halifax, 2009) was created by Toronto-based Theatrefront's collective, The Ensemble, and directed by Daryl Cloran. The bilingual work, which utilised physical and text-based theatre, came out of a development workshop co-produced in 2005 with the Baxter Theatre Centre, Cape Town, and further workshops in Toronto with the South African artists. In 2012 the work toured Western Canada. The word 'ubuntu' refers to the idea that a person is constituted by their relationship to a community or collectivity, and Cloran's production offered a utopian vision of transcontinental interdependency and shared history between Canada and South Africa, centring on a South African protagonist travelling to Canada to find his father. A work like *Ubuntu* owes a certain theatrical debt to the renaissance of African Canadian theatre, spearheaded in the 1990s and early 2000s by Djanet Sears, whose celebrated *Harlem Duet* (Tarragon Theatre, Toronto, 1997) brought African diasporic history and culture into a wider field of vision. What makes *Ubuntu* distinctive is that it required participants to negotiate geo-political as well as cultural borders.

Toronto today has one of the highest intakes of immi-grants of any city in the West. Doug Saunders argues that it 'may be the world's most complete collection of ... old style arrival cities' (*Arrival City*, p. 317), areas that were formerly marginal sites of arrival but have been incorpo-rated into the economic and cultural life of the city. Toronto is also promoted, as Ric Knowles observes, as 'the world's most multicultural city', and 'the third most active theatre center in the English-speaking world' ('Multicultural Text, Intercultural Performance', 2009, p. 73). This image is linked to Canada's official multiculturalism, which, Knowles argues, has tended in various ways since the 1970s to award arts funding that supports cultural preservation projects, keeping 'othered cultures in their static, nostalgic, and dehistoricized ethnic place', while 'large "mainstream" companies in Toronto, complying with the multicultural script, fill the "diversity slots" in their seasons with "ethnic" exotica' (p. 78). Of course, plenty of work modifies the script. The following paragraphs offer a glimpse of what Knowles (drawing on the work of performance scholar Baz Kershaw) describes as Toronto's 'interdependent ecology of intercultural performance' (p. 74), robust in its diversity and constantly reconfiguring itself in response to – and with – its newest arrivals.

Jumblies Theatre is an organisation that works within some of Toronto's multicultural communities, facilitating collaboration between professionals and non-professionals as well as mentoring emerging artists. The company's musical production *Bridge of One Hair* (Harbourfront Centre, Toronto, 2007), which takes its name from a Scottish fairytale, was scripted by founding artistic director Ruth Howard, with a score by Alice Ping Yee Ho. The production was directed by Faye Dupras and based on the work of Toronto-based Somali oral poet Hawa Jibril. *Bridge of One Hair* was as much a process as a theatrical product: it grew from Jumblies's three-year residency in west Toronto's Etobicoke district, which is made up of almost 50 per cent foreign-born residents, and involved refugees and migrants from the Mabelle housing complex in Etobicoke. Over the course of the residency, participants (adults and children) produced performances, installations and folk art.

More recently, Jumblies created *Like an Old Tale* (Commercial Studios, Toronto, 2011), a participatory production directed by Varrick Grimes and adapted from Shakespeare's *The Winter's Tale*, involving Tamil and Nipissing First Nation communities in the deprived neighbourhood of East Scarborough, where more than half of residents are foreign-born. Like *Bridge of One Hair*, the project was process-oriented. More than 400 people got involved over the course of Jumblies's three-year residency and workshop series in East Scarborough, which culminated in an interactive installation in addition to the production at a former film studio. The latter was performed by a large cast of adults and children and used dance, puppetry and mask, projection and choral singing. The space was configured informally, with spectators seated at tables, so invitations to participate were more akin to creative interaction than to crossing a line into the 'stage' space.

Boat stories have been peppered throughout this book, and Canada has its share. In 2011, Toronto's Why Not Theatre produced a site-specific podcast performance, *No Entry: Stories from the MV Sun Sea*, in response to the arrival on the British Columbian coast in 2010 of a derelict cargo ship carrying 492 Sri Lankan Tamil asylum seekers, which provoked debates about how long individuals can be detained while their asylum applications are in process. Directed by Ravi Jain, *No Entry* used testimonies from the asylum seekers and from Sri Lankan Canadian advocates. Audience members listened through headphones to stories that concentrated on how and why individuals fled and their experiences upon arrival in Canada. The work was connected to another of Why Not Theatre's projects, which was concerned to recuperate the history of the Japanese ship *Komagata Maru*, whose 376 British Indian passengers were refused entry upon arrival in Canada in 1914. Both projects challenged celebratory images of Canadian multiculturalism by juxtaposing stories, separated by almost 100 years, of suspicion and rejection of migrants deemed undesirable.

London, Cape Town and Toronto show up one of the key consequences of theatre of migration in contemporary cities: engagement with the dominant 'scripts', in Knowles's sense of the term, or 'strategies', in de Certeau's sense, that define them. These cities' theatres of migration are sometimes congruent with and sometimes countervail the interests of, respectively, London's expertly packaged diversity, Cape Town's post-segregation organisation of space and Toronto's state-sanctioned multiculturalism.

Conclusion

The range, selective as it is, of theatre and performance discussed in this book is indicative of the fact that migration means different things to different people. It can mean mythologies of settler tenacity, or the tracing of ancestral origins back to, variously, the slave trade, convict transportation or the gold rush. It can mean histories of post-war borderlines, or commonwealth immigration to former imperial centres. It can mean the displacement of indigenous people, the resettlement of refugees, or memories of removal and return among those uprooted by segregation. Interwoven with all these is migration as myth and metaphor: the travails of Odysseus or of Rama and Sita.

Migration may mean different things to different people, but I want to suggest that the most politically and artistically satisfying theatres of migration are those that manage to push beyond unexamined metaphors, particularly the slippage that generalises a human condition in which the estrangement of the migrant is equated with the interior nomadism of any person who seeks to distance themselves from cultural, social or national conventions. Theatre and performance that can show audiences some of the conditions and circumstances in which literal migrations occur resists what Sara Ahmed, in an incisive analysis of the subject, describes as the 'migrant ontology [that] works as a form of humanism – we are all migrants' (*Strange Encounters*, p. 84). If we can start to disentangle geographical movement from humanist metaphor, refugee from traveller, person from mythic hero, we may reach solid ground for exploring the very real psycho-affective pull and the aesthetic pleasures that come from their entanglement in the first place.

As the work I've looked at shows, a lot of theatre of migration coalesces around notions of *home*. As soon as one becomes a migrant, home becomes a problem. If we attempt to pin down what home means, we can say that it is simultaneously a location, an idea (which may be consigned to memory) and a material and affective practice (of being 'at home', with people, things and behaviours). When local populations encounter migrants, certain convictions are triggered about who may be allowed to enact a 'homely' relationship with a place. In *Routes: Travel and Translation in the Late Twentieth Century* (1997), James Clifford argues that '[o]nce traveling is foregrounded as a cultural practice, then dwelling, too, needs to be reconceived' (p. 44). Travel of the kind Clifford describes can be thought of as a temporary migration (and with its increasing ubiquity, it's probably one of the keys to empathic understanding between migrants and their audiences). In theatre and performance that concerns itself with more permanent forms of migration it is arguably even more vital that artists and audiences think through dwelling. And part of this is the extent to which dwelling is helped or hindered by hosts, who are already home.

further reading

To date, no other book in English has dealt directly with theatre and migration, but recent books on exile and performance offer further reading on a cognate topic. Yana Meerzon's *Performing Exile, Performing Self: Drama, Theatre, Film* (2012) is a theorised account of the careers of six contemporary artists that is particularly concerned with the psycho-affective dimensions of estrangement and creativity. In the context of nation, Meerzon's edited collection, with Silvija Jestrovic, *Performance, Exile and 'America'* (2009), offers insights into the complex and diverse American 'chronotope' of exile.

Books on minority, intercultural and intracultural theatres intersect with issues of migration. In Britain, Graham Ley and Sarah Dadswell's edited books *British South Asian Theatres: A Documented History* and *Critical Essays on British South Asian Theatre*, both published in 2012, are timely. Geoffrey V. Davis and Anne Fuchs's edited collection *Staging*

New Britain: Aspects of Black and South Asian British Theatre Practice (2006) and Dominic Hingorani's monograph *British Asian Theatre: Dramaturgy, Process and Performance* (2010) trace the work of companies, directors and playwrights. In the Australasian sphere, Helen Gilbert and Jacqueline Lo's *Performance and Cosmopolitics: Cross-cultural Transactions in Australasia* (2007) illuminates theatrical cultural contact in the region, with an emphasis on Aboriginal and Asian engagement. In the context of Asian and Asian-influenced performing arts, Matthew Isaac Cohen's *Performing Otherness: Java and Bali on International Stages, 1905–1952* (2010) recuperates the careers of itinerant artists.

Scholarship on performance of and about asylum seekers and refugees is a burgeoning field. In 2008, Helen Gilbert and Sophie Nield edited a special issue of the British journal *RIDE: Research in Drama Education* (13.2), dedicated to performance and asylum. *Refugee Performance*, edited by Michael Balfour (2013) is a large and wide-ranging collection of new and republished essays. Alison Jeffers's *Refugees, Theatre and Crisis: Performing Global Identities* (2012) provides fresh insights into refugee theatre and performance from around the world.

Agamben, Giorgio. *Means without End: Notes on Politics*. Trans. Vincenzo Binetti and Cesare Casarino. Minneapolis: U of Minnesota P, 2000.

Ahmed, Sara. *Strange Encounters: Embodied Others in Post-Coloniality*. London: Routledge, 2000.

Al-Qady, Towfiq. *Nothing but Nothing. Staging Asylum: Contemporary Australian Plays about Refugees*. Ed. Emma Cox. Sydney: Currency, 2013. 185–202.

Anderson, Benedict. *Imagined Communities: Reflections on the Origin and Spread of Nationalism*. Rev. ed. London: Verso, 1991.

Ang, Ien. *On Not Speaking Chinese: Living between Asia and the West*. London: Routledge, 2001.

Balfour, Michael, ed. *Refugee Performance: Practical Encounters*. Chicago, IL: U of Chicago P, 2013.

Bhabha, Homi K. *The Location of Culture*. London: Routledge, 1994.

Bharucha, Rustom. *The Politics of Cultural Practice: Thinking through Theatre in an Age of Globalization*. London: Athlone, 2000.

Boym, Svetlana. 'Estrangement as a Lifestyle: Shklovsky and Brodsky.' *Poetics Today* 17.4 (1996): 511–30.

Certeau, Michel de. *The Practice of Everyday Life*. Trans. Steven F. Rendall. Berkeley: U of California P, 1984.

Cixous, Hélène. 'Notes on the Program.' *Lincoln Center Festival 2005*. New York, 2005.

Clifford, James. *Routes: Travel and Translation in the Late Twentieth Century*. Cambridge, MA: Harvard UP, 1997.

Cohen, Matthew Isaac. *Performing Otherness: Java and Bali on International Stages, 1905–1952*. Basingstoke, UK: Palgrave Macmillan, 2010.

———. *The Komedie Stamboel: Popular Theater in Colonial Indonesia, 1891–1903*. Athens: Ohio UP, 2006.

Cohen, Robin. *Global Diasporas: An Introduction*. 2nd ed. London: Routledge, 2008.

Cox, Emma. 'Sovereign Ontologies in Australia and Aotearoa–New Zealand: Indigenous Responses to Asylum Seekers, Refugees and Overstayers.' *Knowing Differently: The Cognitive Challenge of the Indigenous*. Ed. G. N. Devy, Geoffrey V. Davis, and K. K. Chakravarty. New Delhi: Routledge, 2013. 139–57.

———. 'Territories of Contact: Two Australian Asylum Seeker Documentaries.' *Moving Worlds: A Journal of Transcultural Writings* 12.2 (2012): 16–29.

———. 'Victimhood, Hope and the Refugee Narrative: Affective Dialectics in Magnet Theatre's *Every Year, Every Day, I Am Walking*.' *Theatre Research International* 37.2 (2012): 118–33.

Cummings, Scott T. 'Real Children and Other Quandaries.' *Hot Review. org: Hunter On-line Theater Review*, Jan. 2003. <http://www.hotreview.org/articles/real-children.htm>.

Davis, Geoffrey V., and Anne Fuchs, eds. *Staging New Britain: Aspects of Black and South Asian British Theatre Practice*. Brussels: Peter Lang, 2006.

Davis, Jack. *No Sugar. Australia Plays: New Australian Drama*. Ed. and introd. Katharine Brisbane. London: Nick Hern, 1989. 179–278.

Dunkelberg, Kermit. '*Children of Herakles*.' *Theatre Journal* 55.3 (2003): 538–39.

Euripides. *Iphigenia in Tauris*. Ed., trans., and commentary by M. J. Cropp. Warminster, UK: Aris & Phillips, 2000.

Flockemann, Miki, Wahseema Roberts, Andrea Castle, Antjie Krog, and Kudzayi Ngara. 'Performing Xenophobia: A Conversation with Jonathan Nkala and Bo Petersen.' *South African Theatre Journal* 23.1 (2009): 207–20.

Fragkou, Marissia. '"Other" Stories: Action, Ethics, Citizenship.' *Contemporary Theatre Review* backpages 21.3 (2011): 371–73.

Fugard, Athol. *The Township Plays: No-Good Friday; Nongogo; The Coat; Sizwe Bansi Is Dead; The Island*. Oxford: Oxford UP, 1993.

Garbutt, Rob. 'Towards an Ethics of Location.' *Landscapes of Exile: Once Perilous, Now Safe*. Ed. Anna Haebich and Baden Offord. Bern: Peter Lang, 2008. 175–92.

Gilbert, Helen, and Jacqueline Lo. *Performance and Cosmopolitics: Cross-cultural Transactions in Australasia*. Basingstoke, UK: Palgrave Macmillan, 2007.

Gilbert, Helen, and Sophie Nield, eds. Performance and Asylum: Ethics, Embodiment, Community. Spec. issue of *RIDE: Research in Drama Education* 13.2 (2008).

Goodman, James. 'Refugee Solidarity: Between National Shame and Global Outrage.' *Theorizing Emotions: Sociological Explorations and Applications*. Ed. Debra Hopkins, Jochen Kleres, Helena Flam, and Helmut Kuzmics. Frankfurt: Campus, 2009. 269–89.

Gorman, Robert. 'Poets, Playwrights and the Politics of Exile and Asylum in Ancient Greece and Rome.' *International Journal of Refugee Law* 6.3 (1994): 402–24.

Grehan, Helena. *Performance, Ethics and Spectatorship in a Global Age*. Basingstoke, UK: Palgrave Macmillan, 2009.

Gunew, Sneja. 'The Home of Language: A Pedagogy of the Stammer.' *Uprootings/Regroundings: Questions of Home and Migration*. Ed. Sara Ahmed, Claudia Castañeda, Anne-Marie Fortier, and Mimi Sheller. Oxford: Berg, 2003. 41–58.

Gutthy, Agnieszka, ed. *Exile and the Narrative/Poetic Imagination*. Newcastle upon Tyne, UK: Cambridge Scholars, 2010.

Hingorani, Dominic. *British Asian Theatre: Dramaturgy, Process and Performance*. Basingstoke, UK: Palgrave Macmillan, 2010.

Huang, Alexander C. Y. 'The Theatricality of Religious Rhetoric: Gao Xingjian and the Meaning of Exile.' *Theatre Journal* 63.3 (2011): 365–79.

Hutchison, Yvette. 'Verbatim Theatre in South Africa: "Living History in a Person's Performance".' *Get Real: Documentary Theatre Past and Present*. Ed. Alison Forsyth and Chris Megson. Basingstoke, UK: Palgrave Macmillan, 2009. 209–23.

Huynh, Kim. 'Refugeeness: What's Good and Not So Good about Being Persecuted and Displaced?' *Local–Global* 8 (2010): 52–74.

Janaczewska, Noëlle. *Songket and This Territory*. Sydney: Currency, 2008.

Jeffers, Alison. *Refugees, Theatre and Crisis: Performing Global Identities*. Basingstoke, UK: Palgrave Macmillan, 2012.

Jestrovic, Silvija, and Yana Meerzon. *Performance, Exile and 'America'*. Basingstoke, UK: Palgrave Macmillan, 2009.

John, Errol. *Moon on a Rainbow Shawl*. London: Faber, 1958.

Kardas-Nelson, Mara. 'Kaapse Klopse Still March to Their Own Beat.' *Mail and Guardian* [Johannesburg] 4 Jan. 2013. <http://mg.co.za/article/2013-01-04-00-kaapse-klopse-still-march-to-their-own-beat>.

Kelly, Veronica. *The Empire Actors: Stars of Australian Costume Drama*. Sydney: Currency House, 2011.

Knowles, Ric. 'Multicultural Text, Intercultural Performance: The Performance Ecology of Contemporary Toronto.' *Performance and the City*. Ed. D. J. Hopkins, Shelley Orr, and Kim Solga. Basingstoke, UK: Palgrave Macmillan, 2009. 73–91.

Laera, Margherita. 'Reaching Athens: Performing Participation and Community in Rimini Protokoll's *Prometheus in Athens*.' *Performance Research: A Journal of the Performing Arts* 16.4 (2011): 46–51.

Lawler, Ray. *Summer of the Seventeenth Doll*. London: Angus and Robertson, 1957.

Ley, Graham, and Sarah Dadswell, eds. *British South Asian Theatres: A Documented History*. Exeter: U of Exeter P, 2012.

———. *Critical Essays on British South Asian Theatre*. Exeter: U of Exeter P, 2012.

Mazower, David. *Yiddish Theatre in London*. London: The Jewish Museum, 1987.

Meerzon, Yana. *Performing Exile, Performing Self: Drama, Theatre, Film*. Basingstoke, UK: Palgrave Macmillan, 2012.

Moreton-Robinson, Aileen. 'I Still Call Australia Home: Indigenous Belonging and Place in a White Postcolonizing Society.' *Uprootings/ Regroundings: Questions of Home and Migration*. Ed. Sara Ahmed, Claudia Castañeda, Anne-Marie Fortier, and Mimi Sheller. Oxford: Berg, 2003. 23–40.

Morreira, Shannon. 'Seeking Solidarity: Zimbabwean Undocumented Migrants in Cape Town, 2007.' *Journal of Southern African Studies* 36.2 (2010): 433–48.

Nancy, Jean-Luc. *The Inoperative Community*. Ed. and trans. Peter Connor. Minneapolis: U of Minnesota P, 1991.

Needa, Veronica. *FACE: Renegotiating Identity through Performance*. MA diss. University of Kent, 2009.

Nkala, Jonathan. *The Crossing*. Theatre in Translation Online Library Text 8.1, 2011.

Nowra, Louis. *The Golden Age. Australia Plays: New Australian Drama*. Introd. Katharine Brisbane. London: Nick Hern, 1989. 89–178.

Pirie, Gordon. 'Reanimating a Comatose Goddess: Reconfiguring Central Cape Town.' *Urban Forum* 18 (2007): 125–51.

Sandrow, Nahma. *Vagabond Stars: A World History of Yiddish Theater*. Syracuse, NY: Syracuse UP, 1995.

Saunders, Doug. *Arrival City*. London: Windmill, 2011.

Shewey, Don. 'Peter Sellars's CNN Euripides.' *The Village Voice: Theater* 28 Jan. 2003. <http://www.villagevoice.com/2003-01-28/theater/peter-sellars-s-cnn-euripides/full/>.

Sontag, Susan. *Regarding the Pain of Others*. London: Penguin, 2003.

Stephensen, P. R. 'The Foundations of Culture in Australia: An Essay towards National Self-Respect.' Gordon, NSW: W.J. Miles, 1936.

UNHCR. '2014 UNHCR Country Operations Profile – South Africa.'
    <http://www.unhcr.org/pages/49e485aa6.html>.

Verma, Jatinder. '"Braids" and Theatre Practice.' *EnterText* 2.1 (2001):
    125–40.

Western, John. *Outcast Cape Town*. Rev. ed. Berkeley: U of California P,
    1996.

index